D0821535

VERNON BARTLETT was described by Harold Nicolson in the *Observer* as 'a famous broadcaster . . . twice elected to Parliament . . . one of the most influential foreign correspondents there has ever been . . . on intimate terms with many of his eminent contemporaries'.

Mr. Bartlett has written about the experiences of his eventful career in his three volumes of autobiography—*This Is My Life, And Now, Tomorrow* and *Tuscan Retreat*. He has written two travel books, *A Book about Elba* (now in its second edition) and *Introduction to Italy*. He now lives at Lucca in Italy.

THE PAST OF PASTIMES

By the same author

*

CALF LOVE
TOPSY TURVY
UNKNOWN SOLDIER
THIS IS MY LIFE
TOMORROW ALWAYS COMES
GO EAST, OLD MAN
STRUGGLE FOR AFRICA
REPORT FROM MALAYA
AND NOW, TOMORROW
TUSCAN RETREAT
A BOOK ABOUT ELBA
INTRODUCTION TO ITALY
ETC.

THE PAST OF PASTIMES

Vernon Bartlett

1969
ARCHON BOOKS

This edition first published
in the United States
by
Archon Books, 1969

SBN 208 00936 1

© Vernon Bartlett 1969

Printed in Great Britain by
R. & R. Clark, Ltd, Edinburgh
Scotland

Contents

Illustrations

6

ILLUSTRATIONS

ILLUSTRATIONS

The publishers gladly acknowledge the assistance of Illustration Research Service in compiling the illustrations for this book.

Plates 1, 5a, 6b, 14a and 14b are reproduced from photographs by R. B. Fleming; plates 6c, 13a and 13b from photographs by John R. Freeman; plates 7a, 7b and 16 from photographs by Rodney Todd-White; plate 9 from a photograph by Matter and Weich, Cape Town.

Acknowledgements

I am grateful to the authors of the books listed in the bibliography, who have helped me without knowing that they were doing so. My thanks go still more to those others who have consciously and deliberately sacrificed some of their time on my behalf, and in particular to Miss Diana Rait Kerr, Curator of the Marylebone Cricket Club; Mrs Alix Wilkinson of the Department of Egyptian Antiquities, British Museum; Mr R. C. Haines of Messrs Slazenger; and Mr Anthony Peek, Stage Director of the Theatre Royal, Haymarket. Mrs Joan St G. Saunders, of Writer's and Speaker's Research, deserves a sentence of thanks all to herself.

V.B.

CHAPTER ONE

Leisure and Rubber

The problem of leisure · 'The gumme which cometh from a tree' · Bread and circuses · 'Featheries' and 'gutties' · The contents of tennis and golf balls

THE peg on which I had proposed to hang this book isn't there. But half of the book had been written before a young lady of great charm and intimidating knowledge, in the Department of Egyptian Antiquities of the British Museum, explained this to me. It seemed nevertheless sensible to go ahead, peg or no peg.

I had read somewhere that, among the articles found in the tomb of Queen Hatshepsut who reigned in Egypt in the sixteenth century B.C., had been some dice. Not ordinary dice, but loaded dice. The idea of sending a queen on her way to heaven with loaded dice to help her when she got there so appealed to me that I began to read everything I could find about the history and continuity of sports and pastimes. When I had done this for several months, I visited London and hurried off to the British Museum, where Hatshepsut's dice were alleged to be. The young lady to whom I appealed for help was sympathetic, but she assured me that dice do not seem to have been known in Egypt before Ptolemaic times, a mere three or four centuries before Christ.

A book begun in so haphazard a way is obviously not a very serious one. It does not pretend to deal with all the major sports and pastimes. It does not give you the rules by which you can play this game or that. It is no more than a random collection of facts or statements which, it is hoped, may amuse or enlighten the reader. But I realise that in two respects the nature of my subject is of increasing importance.

In the first place, there is the increasing seriousness with which people take their sports and games. A few years ago, the poor show put up by the Italian team in the struggle for Association Football's World Cup was treated so much as a national disaster that there were angry debates about it in the Italian parliament. The success of the British team, on the other hand, was considered sufficiently important to justify the issue of a special set of postage stamps. Recently, in the West Indies, the habit of throwing broken bottles at players has spread even to the cricket field. Girls despairingly lose their hope of becoming swimming champions because their bosoms develop, and they are no longer sufficiently stream-lined. In Singapore, I used to watch would-be swimming champions in training. There they were, boys and girls in their early teens, doing their daily fifty lengths of the pool, or diving flat on their stomachs in a way that would have aroused sympathetic laughter at their 'belly-flops' when I was a boy, but that nowadays must be endured so that they do not waste valuable seconds under-water at the beginning of a race. These children had no time to play the fool, as most of us tend to do when we get into water above our knees. The time for childish behaviour would come, if at all, when they were middle-aged or old; now they had their championships to worry about. And so it is with almost every outdoor game – the amateur, who played to amuse himself, has been replaced by the professional, who has his living to earn. On the very day when I sat down to write these words, I read in the *Observer* this statement by Mr Herman David, chairman of the All-England Club: 'The only straight people left in lawn tennis are the professionals, who earn their money honestly and openly.' And now Wimbledon welcomes these professionals.

In another and much more important respect my subject is a serious one. Scientists are rightly proud of their inventiveness in relieving mankind of many forms of drudgery. But sociologists are rightly worried by the fact that automation, computers and all the rest of it will soon face us with a problem of leisure that may be even more difficult to solve than the problem of feeding too many people on too small a globe. Not being a sociologist, I do not know in what proportions the juvenile delinquency in the countries we like to consider as the most civilised is due to the cinema, the world wars, the decay of religion or the 'telly'. But, remembering the time when I and my fellow thugs—all under twelve—broke the glass of every lamp-post in Branksome Chine, I am convinced that a large share of the blame should go to boredom, sheer boredom. I had not then such distractions as the cinema and the radio, and I suspect that I abandoned gangsterism when I was given my first bicycle—an affair with a fixed wheel, so that I had to mount it by hopping along on one foot with the other foot on a 'step' projecting from the rear hub. In any case, my boredom was probably less intense, since I had to devise my own pastimes, than is that of today's children, to whom the 'do it yourself' craze is a stimulating innovation.

But what about the future, when computers will have replaced millions of workers, when factories will produce all our food in the dismal form of plankton pills, when cars will have been replaced by hovercraft and helicopters, when we shall be able to absorb knowledge without troubling to read a book? I look at the statues of kings or generals on prancing horses and of statesmen in uncomfortable frock coats, and wonder what sort of men, if any, will be commemorated by statues in the future. At least in the more advanced countries, they are unlikely to be war leaders, for there is nothing romantic about a napalm bomb. Some, no doubt, will be reformers, but not many, for reformers are apt to be very earnest men, unimpressive in physique and lacking popular appeal. Will not the majority, I ask myself, be men whom our parents would have condemned as wastrels, men whom we were advised to avoid because they would encourage us to waste our time? Are not these men, in fact, the benefactors of mankind? Is it not a scandal that, even to this day, no statue exists to keep alive the memory of such a man as Sir Henry Wickham?

Wickham? Who was he? If you don't know, nor does one in fifty of your neighbours. And yet, according to the new standards which science is compelling us to adopt, he was one of the greatest pioneers of history. Neither of my encyclopaedias devotes even a paragraph to him, although he made so spectacular a contribution to man's comfort and to his pleasant use of leisure.

In 1876, with the connivance of Sir Joseph Hooker, Director of Kew Gardens, Wickham went out to Brazil and, after considerable adventures and successful smuggling, brought back about 70,000 seeds of the rubber tree to England. Some of these were germinated at Kew and the saplings were sent out to Ceylon and Malaysia—in the Malayan town of Kuala Kangsar, you can still see a few of these original saplings in their moss-covered old age. The Brazilians, not surprisingly, were furious, but the British were characteristically slow to appreciate the service that Wickham had rendered them. Thirty-five years went by before, at a dinner in his honour, he was presented by Kew with a cheque for a thousand guineas and some plate. It was not until 1920 that a knighthood was conferred on this man who may be said to have started the rubber industry upon which, quite literally, most of the world's trade and traffic moves.

Of course, many people before Wickham had noticed the resilient qualities of rubber. Columbus himself is said to have been amazed by natives of Haiti playing with a ball 'made of a gum tree' which bounced in a way

he had never witnessed before. Hernan Cortes, the
Spanish conqueror of Mexico early in the sixteenth
century, found the Mexicans playing with a ball of 'the
gumme which cometh from a tree'. But to Wickham
goes the credit for foreseeing some of the potentialities
of this white, milky substance called latex, found in
many plants but above all in the *Hevea brasiliensis*, the
trees which have replaced so many thousands of acres
of Asian and African tropical jungle. Among the results
of his foresight, dozens of governments have been able
to balance their budgets, hundreds of business men have
made fortunes, and—perhaps even more important—
millions of people have solved the problem of what to do
with their spare time by playing games or by watching
others play games. The present world production of
golf balls is rather more than ninety millions a year, and
that of tennis balls is about twenty-five millions. What
would the world be like today had there been no Henry
Wickham? And what will it be like fifty years from now
unless other benefactors have discovered other ways of
occupying the attention of far more people with far
more empty hours to fill?

*   *   *

The problem is not so new as we are apt to think,
although it is certainly far more urgent than ever before.
It worried the Roman emperors, for example, and under-
lined the importance of their *panem et circenses*. Without
plenty of bread and circuses, the Romans would have
become politically restless because they had little to do
and much time in which to do it. Each military campaign produced thousands of slaves to do all the dirty
work. Pliny the Younger, friend of the Emperor Trajan
in the first century A.D., had some five hundred slaves,
and Roman citizens were discouraged from doing most
kinds of work even more vehemently than members of

the British aristocracy were discouraged from 'trade' in the last century. In Imperial Rome at least half the population drew a free daily ration of wheat, and at least half the days of the year were public holidays. What could the people do with so much leisure? The chariot races in the Circus Maximus became more and more impressive, and in some cases there were eight to ten horses to each chariot; the contests in the arenas became increasingly brutal and cruel—when the Emperor Titus inaugurated the Colosseum five thousand beasts are said to have been killed in one day. Were this a very serious book, I should be tempted to speculate whether the cultivation of violence in our entertainments of today is not disquietingly similar to Roman entertainments during the long period of decadence. But this is not a very serious book.

*   *   *

Historians differ as to the identity of the man who invented the first ball, which is not surprising, since he must have been one of our remotest ancestors. The instinct to kick an object lying on the ground is a very strong one, quickly checked by the discovery that a round stone is an uncomfortable object for a bare-footed man to kick. (Less uncomfortable, perhaps, than most of us would expect; one of the most vigorous games of football I ever watched was played on the *padang* at Malacca between teams of bare-footed Chinese and bare-footed Indians.)

Herodotus, 'the father of history', who wrote more than four centuries before the birth of Christ, claimed that the ball had been invented by a most remarkable people, the Lydians, who are credited with the invention of almost every pastime except chess, and about whom I shall write in the next chapter. According to other writers, the first woman who made a ball to play with was called Anagalla, on the Greek island of Corcyra; she gave the ball to Nausicaa, the king's daughter, and Homer described her, in the *Odyssey*, playing with her girl friends. As in many other games, something that at first was looked upon as suitable only for women and children was subsequently adopted and adapted by men for their own more vigorous pursuits.

How did the enthusiastic manage before they had followed the example of primitive American Indians and had learnt to use balls made of rubber? The early tennis balls were made of leather and stuffed with feathers, human hair or wool waste. The game of tennis originated in France, and several French kings were enthusiastic players. In 1480, Louis XI decreed that tennis balls must be stuffed with wool wadding, 'and not containing sand, ground chalk, metal shavings, lime, bran, sawdust, ash, moss, powder or earth'. As early as 1292, there were at least thirteen manufacturers of tennis balls in Paris.

The first golf balls were known as 'featheries', and were made of boiled soft feathers – 'as many as would fill the brim of a top hat' – which were pushed through a small hole in a leather sphere. This sphere was then sewn up, hammered until it was quite round, and painted. The first 'gutties', or balls of gutta percha, were made in Scotland in 1845, the gutta percha being cut into strips, softened in hot water, and then rolled by hand. They aroused the angry opposition of many players, and especially of Allan Robertson, ball-maker at St Andrews, who had made nearly 2,500 'featheries' in the previous year. He bribed the caddies to bring him all the 'gutties' they found, so that he could 'burn the filth'.

But even this 'filth' was soon out-dated; an American, Coburn Haskell, invented rubber-cored balls in 1898. Golf balls with liquid centres were first made in 1907, and have changed little since that year, although I am told by Messrs Slazenger that in 1946 the United States Golf Association introduced a maximum velocity rule, the aim of which is to prevent the manufacture of balls that can be hit too far since they tend to make the courses too short. From the same expert source I learn that 'from a normal club-head speed of 110 miles per hour, the ball will travel off the tee at 150 m.p.h., with an initial backward spin of 3,500 to 4,000 revolutions per minute. The club is slowed to approximately 85 m.p.h. after contact, the contact time being only one half-thousandth of a second. In this time, the energy absorbed by the ball is equivalent to a horse-power of three hundred.'

Thank Heaven I gave up golf!

*   *   *

This is a book about the past of pastimes (and I use the word as though it were written 'pass-times', since an interest even in such important events as the Davis Cup Final, the Test Matches, the World Series Baseball contests, or the Cresta Run Grand National is, in the last resort, merely a way of passing the time). Who first laid down the rules of polo? Who made the first skates? Who invented 'Snakes and Ladders'? Why do the Americans play with a 'deck' of cards, and the British with a 'pack'? Who invented draughts, and who gave it so strange a name? Who first worked out the mathematics of a roulette wheel? How does it happen that the children of so many different countries play such similar games?

At the time of writing this preliminary chapter, I know the answers to few of these and other questions that crowd into the mind. I suspect that to some of them I shall find no satisfactory answers at all, since I do not intend to spend the remaining years of my life in research. But I hope to come across enough unexpected in-

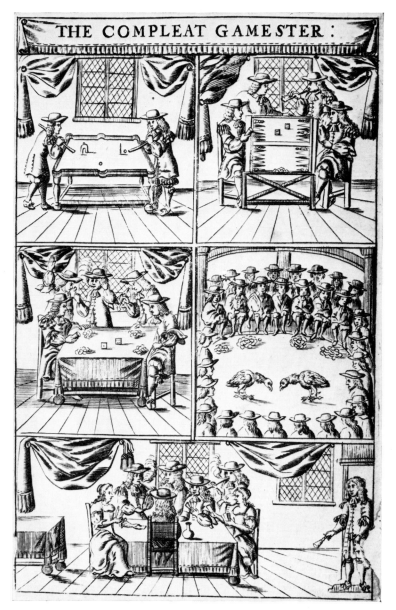

1 Frontispiece to *The Compleat Gamester* by Charles Cotton

2(a) Egyptian ball game, 1900 B.C.

2(b) Who invented hockey? A Greek ball game (p. 47)

formation to amuse a reasonable number of readers; in any case I shall have found a pleasant pastime for myself in reading so many books on the subject. And any embarrassment I might otherwise have felt about passing on the results of other people's labours has been removed by someone who recently reminded me that, whereas the act of taking material from one book is condemned as plagiarism, the act of taking material from many is lauded as research.

CHAPTER TWO

The Delights of Dice

*Four categories of games· The invention of dice·'Craps' and hazard·
How to load your dice· The slow boat to China· Gambling in early
times· The game of* mora

GAMES and pastimes can be divided, very roughly,
into four categories. There are those which enable
us physically to let off steam, to show more muscular
prowess than our competitors, to run faster, to dive
more gracefully, to climb higher, to drive farther down
the fairway than they can. There are those, such as
chess, bridge or even scrabble, which keep the brain
alert. There are those which aim to do no more than
avoid boredom. There are those which are designed less
to pass the time pleasantly than to win something,
probably money, from somebody else.

One cannot, of course, draw a clear and definite line
between one category and another. For example, it is
well known that such games as rummy are games of
chance when you are losing and games of skill when you
are winning. Most games of dice are played in order to
win something from somebody else, but many of them
really come in the category of games that are designed
to avoid boredom. Even that most pleasant of holidays—
a voyage on a slow boat to China—might become dull
unless, before lunch and before dinner, there were that
meeting in the bar to decide who is to pay for the next
round of drinks. If the idea of winning a drink from
your neighbour were all that mattered, it could be decided by one throw of the dice. Instead, everyone has
five matches or so which have to be lost before the decision can be reached. The drinks, indeed, are often far

ahead of the dice-throw that will decide who is to pay
for them. It could therefore be argued that the dice tend
to slow down the drinking, and should be welcomed by
those who want everybody else to abjure alcohol—not a
very honest or convincing argument, perhaps, but nor
are many other arguments about much more serious
subjects.

*   *   *

Dice have been played since very early times. The
word comes from the Latin, *dare*—to give. (In my case,
I think, more often given by me to others than by
others to me.) At least three Roman emperors—
Augustus, Nero and Claudius—were great dice players,
and Claudius even wrote a book on the subject. In a
letter quoted by Suetonius, Augustus wrote: 'Yesterday
and today, as is our custom, we threw dice during our
meals.' Caligula, another imperial player, was notorious
for his cheating. Mark Antony played dice in Alex-
andria in the intervals when he was not making love to
Cleopatra. But people were rattling dice in dice-boxes
several centuries before the competitive instinct drove
Romulus to kill his brother Remus during the first
building of Rome.

Who, then, invented dice? The Greek, Palamedes, is
said to have done so to keep his soldiers occupied during
the siege of Troy, about 1184 B.C. The legend I prefer
attributes their invention to King Atys, who ruled over
the people of Lydia, Asia Minor, during a long period
of famine. According to Herodotus, Atys allowed the
people to eat on one day, but compelled them to fast
on the next, and to lessen the rigour of the fasting days
he made them play all kinds of games. 'It is said that it
was then that the game of dice, the game of knuckles,
games of ball and other games were invented, but not
the game of draughts, the invention of which the Lydians

do not claim.' It seems quite probable that they invented the cubic dice, several of which have been found in Etruscan tombs. The Lydians lived in this manner, says Herodotus, for eighteen years. Despite this system – or possibly because of it – the famine continued, and Atys had to divide his people into two groups, one under his own command and the other under that of his son. He then drew lots – or threw dice – to decide which group should stay in Lydia and which should emigrate. His son lost, and went with his group down to Smyrna, where they built ships in which they sailed into the west. 'After skirting the shores of many lands', Herodotus continued, 'they reached the land of the Umbrians. There they founded towns, in which they live to this day. But they changed their name of Lydians for another, derived from that of the son of the king who had led them. Taking his name as theirs, they called themselves Tyrrhenians.' And the Tyrrhenians are believed to be none other than the Etruscans, who gave Rome her early kings. The sea between Sardinia and the Italian mainland is still called the Tyrrhenian Sea.

Dice in the early days were not cubes, but were made from knuckle-bones taken from the hind legs of sheep or other cloven-footed animals, and were oblong. Games with these bones or with articles shaped like them were later confined to the women and children (and one of their games is played by British children today, under the name of 'Jacks' or 'Fivestones'); the more sophisticated cubes were reserved for men and their gambling. Is it only a coincidence that Americans talk of 'rolling the bones' when they are throwing craps? Probably, several games of Asian origin were spread across Africa by Arabs in the slave-raiding days. Is it outrageous to suppose that dice, which, in their origin, were bones, were taken to America by Negro slaves?

One tends to associate 'craps' with Negroes throwing dice on a dusty porch in one of the Southern States. The game, however, derives from the French *hazard*, which takes its name from the Arabic '*al zar*', meaning 'the dice'. It became the most popular game in France just after the French Revolution, and at one time it was played in more than thirty gambling houses in the now quiet and respectable Palais Royal in Paris. It also became very popular at Almack's and Crockford's, the London gaming clubs which first became famous in the nineteenth century. Crockford, by the way, was originally a fishmonger, but he found gambling a more remunerative occupation, and when he retired from his club he had a fortune estimated at more than a million sterling, almost all of which he subsequently lost in unfortunate speculations. The Duke of Wellington was one of Crockford's most distinguished members, but he is said to have joined only in order to be able to blackball his son, Lord Douro, should he apply for membership.

The knuckle-bones could fall on one of only four sides, the ends being too convex. These sides were also uneven, and it seems probable that this fact gave them the different values we find on our dice of today. The numbering of dice so that any two opposite sides add up to seven is very ancient, and may go back to the knuckle-bones or astragals of the Greeks. If the rounded part came uppermost, the score was four, and the throw was known as a 'baker'; the concave side was the 'thief', and scored three; the small, flat surface was a 'vizier', and scored only one; the side opposite the 'vizier' was the 'king', and scored six. The Greeks generally played with three dice, and the highest throw—three sixes—was called an 'Aphrodite'; and the Romans, in their turn, called this throw after Venus, their goddess of love. A 'Venus' scooped the pool. In both countries, the lowest throw was a 'dog', which name both Greeks and Egyptians gave to their pawns at chess.

There are dozens of games depending entirely upon dice, and dozens more in which dice play an important part. It is therefore not very surprising that crooks found ways of 'loading' their dice. I have already mentioned my failure to find loaded dice dating back to the reign of Queen Hatshepsut—there were then no dice to load. But Pompeii, which has revealed so much about the lives of the ancient Romans, has revealed dice treated in this way. The favourite trick was to insert minute spots of quicksilver so that the dice would fall with the lowest score downwards. Charles Cotton,* writing in the seventeenth century, knew another method which consisted of 'sticking a hog's bristle so in the corners, or otherwise in the dice' that 'they shall run high or low as they please; this bristle must be strong and short, by which means the bristle bending, it will not lie on the side, but will be tript over'. (This description, I fear, will not greatly help you in your own efforts to load your dice, but perhaps that is just as well.) In Imperial Rome, many players had dice made of Baltic amber or of crystal, and I wonder whether this fashion had anything to do with the fact that bristles or quicksilver would be easier to detect in amber or crystal than in the ivory, precious metals or other opaque materials that were also in use.

Pope Boniface VIII, a pugnacious and energetic pope who ruled for a few months in the year 606, is said to have had the dots on his dice made of gold. One would have thought that he thereby handicapped himself; the six small blobs of gold on one side would surely have so weighted his dice that the opposite side, with only one blob, would fall uppermost. But I find it difficult to be-

* *The Compleat Gamester* (London, 1674)

lieve that so keen a gambler did not somehow correct this disadvantage.

An unexpected use of dice was made by Rabelais, and attributed to one of his characters, a judge named Bridoic. This judge always listened most carefully to the evidence on either side, but at the end of it all he would have the plaintiff's documents piled on one end of a table and those of the defendant piled at the other end. He would then throw the dice to decide in whose favour he should give his verdict. But why, he was asked, had all this evidence been taken before the verdict was reached? *'Pour le forme'*, he replied with dignity.

The sixteenth-century Florentine merchant, Francesco Carletti, whose admirable book on his voyage round the world was published a few years ago, wrote of the Chinese who 'played various games on checkerboards almost like ours, and also one of another kind, with a large number of pieces that make up a large army'. Dice were used in this game, and Carletti describes how 'they pick them up with the points of their fingers and throw them into a porcelain bowl, six at a time, casting them down with an effect and efficacy quite out of the ordinary, and a great waste of time'. Anyone who has watched Americans shooting craps, and talking to their dice while they do so, will appreciate that there are at least some points of similarity between Americans and Chinese, even if one must go back to the sixteenth century to discover them.

There is a Spanish proverb which says that 'the best game of dice is the one you don't play'. Like most proverbs, it is only half true–in view of the tremendous demand for medicines to cure digestive troubles, one might as well say that 'the best meal is the one you don't eat'. Surely dice are good or bad according to the use you make of them. One need not go as far as the Germans, of whom Tacitus wrote in the first century

A.D. that they were 'such gamblers that they would stake their wives, their children, their own liberty. And he who loses submits to servitude, though younger and stronger than his antagonist, and patiently allows himself to be bound and sold in the market place; and this madness they dignify by the name of honour.'

Nor need one emulate the Athenian, Alcibiades, who lived in the fifth century B.C., and who was one of the most impetuous and self-willed leaders in history. Plutarch's life of him gives us what is possibly the first example of a gesture that has been made familiar to us by recent demonstrators against nuclear weapons and other horrific scientific discoveries. As a boy, Alcibiades was gambling with other boys in the street. He threw the dice and they fell in front of an approaching chariot, whose driver refused to stop when called upon to do so; whereupon the boy threw himself full-length on the roadway between the chariot and his dice. One could argue all night as to whether the gambling instinct made him so impetuous or whether his innate impetuosity made him a gambler.

Even a 'high straight' would not induce me to throw myself in the way of an advancing chariot, but I, for one, am grateful to King Atys, to Palamedes, or to whomsoever invented dice. For years—from the Paris Peace Conference of 1919 to the Bandung Conference of 1955—one of my jobs was to cover international conferences for a newspaper. In many cases, I remember less about the decisions they reached or the platitudes which were supposed to conceal the absence of decisions than about the long hours of waiting in the conference building. Why the hell were the delegates so long-winded? Was there time for me to snatch a quick meal before they left the conference room and revealed a few scraps of news before they hurried off to their own dinners? Would I, in any case, have time to write my story in time to catch

the first edition? Was it worth trying to bribe one of the
telephone girls in the hope she would get my call
through to London quickly? Would the call which the
London office was supposed to be putting through to me
come so early that I'd no time to write my story, or so
late that all my colleagues and rivals would have dic-
tated theirs and have gone off for a cheerful midnight
dinner?

How, in such circumstances, could I fail to be grateful
for the gift of dice? How obvious it is that the dice-box,
by making me forget my worries, has prolonged my life
far more than the drinks consumed while I was playing
dice have shortened it! Because I so liked the colleagues with whom I was playing, I enjoyed even so dull
and so prolonged a game as golf dice, in which, with the
aid of the ace as a joker, one sees in how few throws one
can score five aces, five kings, five queens, five jacks,
five tens and five nines.

And on that slow boat from Singapore, when the Suez
crisis sent us home round the Cape of Good Hope,
would I and the eleven other passengers have remained
on such friendly terms without our twice-daily sessions?
Our favourite game was one which is known in polite
society as 'Beat that, my Friend', but by us as 'Beat that,
you Bastard'—after all, we were at sea, and some
dictionaries are alleged to claim that 'bastard' is a 'term
of affection used among sailors'. It is one of those
games in which one hopes to bluff a player into des-
troying himself by rashness, by inducing him to throw
the dice once more, even when the law of averages
clearly advises him not to be such a damned fool. Even
a game so dependent on chance can be defended by the
argument that it helps one to know the characters of
one's fellow-men. Can it?

The same fear of being considered craven is, of
course, the justification of the best of all dicing games—

liar dice. So much depends on your reading of your opponents' characters and upon your own ability to conceal your own feelings. I cannot find anything about the history of liar dice, but I imagine it was invented by passengers on their way to the Far East. I remember being taken, between the two world wars, into a club in Shanghai where there was a large room full of tables, on each of which was an elegant little screen behind which one threw one's dice before trying to persuade one's neighbour that the throw was much higher than, in fact, it was. All gone with the Chinese wind of change!

The Chinese are widely considered to be the world's most inveterate gamblers – and this I can easily believe, having often queued up with them to register my own humble bets at the Singapore race course. But they met their match in Malaya. Guy Wint* refers to the days in the nineteenth century when Chinese labourers were brought to that country to work in the newly-discovered tin mines, and he quotes a British officer who wrote that 'the Malays had a game called *Main China* (the Chinese game), each man betting on the number of coins which a passing Chinese carried in his pouch, and whether they were odd or even. Thereafter, when the bets had been made, they would kill the Chinese and count the coins.'

The passion for dice is very widespread, and I read somewhere that, when the floor of London's Middle Temple was taken up in 1764, the workmen found nearly a hundred dice that had fallen through the cracks between the boards. But people with too much time on their hands do not need even a set of poker dice in their pocket. In Sweden I was once taught a game in which nothing was needed beyond an ordinary matchbox and an ordinary table. You place the box flat on the table

* *The British in Asia* (Faber & Faber, London, 1947)

with one end of the box protruding for about half an inch over the table's edge. With a sharp upward jerk of your finger, you flip the box into the air. If it falls on its back, you score two; if it falls on its side, you score ten; if it falls on its end, you score twenty-five. In each of these cases you have another turn. If it falls on its face, then your turn is over and your score is nil. The past of that particular pastime was, I believe, a long drawn out murder trial in a small and dull Swedish town, and its inventors were newspaper reporters with too much time on their hands.

In Florence, at the time of Dante, towards the end of the thirteenth century, a very popular and rather revealing form of gambling was for each player to put a coin on a wall and wait. The owner of the first coin on which a fly settled took the kitty. The popularity of this pastime suggests that there were plenty of flies in Florence at that time; its nature suggests that it was more akin to robbery than to a game of chance—a finger previously dipped in some sort of syrup and then rubbed on a coin must considerably have affected the odds.

What with their feuds between Guelfs and Ghibellines and their wars with other city states—Lucca, Pisa, Pistoia, Siena and so on, the Florentines in the thirteenth century were passing through one of those periods of uncertainty which generally lead to large-scale gambling. In 1285, for example, and again in 1289, the authorities were seriously worried by *ludus pilae*, or 'the ball game', which consisted of nothing more than throwing a ball against a wall and catching it. This childish activity would seem harmless enough, but the betting on the number of times competitors could catch the ball became so excited and noisy that church services were interrupted and the authorities punished those who took part in it.

Historically, the most interesting form of gambling,

without the use even of a fly, a ball, or a match-box, is the game of *mora*, for which all you need is one hand. Two opponents stand facing each other, each with a fist clenched. Simultaneously each extends one or more fingers and at the same moment calls out his guess at the total of outstretched fingers. If one guesses correctly he has, of course, won the point. Between experts, the game is played so quickly that it gives plenty of possibilities for sleight of hand, and Cicero defined a man of complete integrity as one with whom he could play *mora* in the dark. This was a very popular pastime in ancient Rome; it is still popular in that city's slums; it was popular in Greece and in Egypt before Rome was founded – there are several pictures of it on Egyptian pottery or in Egyptian tombs.

Another variety of this game is called by the Italians *mora cinese* or *mora giapponese* (Chinese or Japanese *mora*). I have seen children playing it in both Peking and Rome, and I imagine that it was brought to Europe by early merchants trading in Chinese silk and porcelain. The players, instead of guessing the number of outstretched fingers, present a clenched fist, two fingers or an open palm. The fist represents a stone; the open palm represents paper; the outstretched fingers represent scissors. The stone is superior to the scissors, since it blunts them. The palm is superior to the stone, since it wraps it up; the scissors are superior to the paper, since they cut it. Apparently both these forms of *mora* are played in most parts of England, and I wonder whether at least the former variety was brought over by Roman legionaries.

One would not expect *mora* to rank very highly as a social amusement, but apparently it was very fashionable as an after-dinner game in ancient Greece.

You never can tell. A famous and very priggish sixteenth-century book on gentlemanly behaviour, *Il*

Libro del Cortegiano, written by Baldassare Castiglione and read in Italian or translation by several generations of young social climbers, stated that the young courtier should know 'how to swim, jump, run, throw stones; for, besides their usefulness in war, it is frequently necessary to show one's prowess in such things, whereby a good name is to be won, especially with the crowd (with whom one must reckon, after all). Another noble exercise, and most suitable for a man at court, is the game of tennis, which shows off the disposition of the body, the quickness and litheness of every member, and all the qualities that are brought out by almost every other form of exercise.'

One might question today the social value of jumping, running, swimming or throwing stones. Tennis, on the other hand has helped many a young man in his career, and still does so. An early example of its value occurred in the sixteenth century, when a young monk who was partnering King Francis I of France won the match with a particularly good stroke. The king said something to the effect that it was a fine stroke for a monk, to which the monk replied: 'Sire, whenever it may please you, it shall be the stroke of an abbot.' An abbey had a vacancy, and the tennis player got the post.

Athletics seem to have played a part in the fifteenth and sixteenth centuries almost comparable with their importance in ancient Greece. With a boastfulness of which one hopes Baldassare would have disapproved, a certain Leon Battisti Alberti claimed that 'with his feet together, he could leap over a man's shoulders; an arrow shot by his hand from his chest could pierce the strongest iron breastplate; he could throw an apple so high into the air that it would go far beyond the tops of the highest roofs'. One wonders about the size of his fish that got away.

CHAPTER THREE

'Real', Lawn and Table Tennis

The invention of tennis · French and British kings as players · No games for the 'lower classes' · 'Real' tennis and lawn tennis · Table tennis and badminton · Wimbledon

PRACTICALLY every ball game has a long history. Our remote ancestors kicked it, and became unwittingly the forefathers of football. They hit it with their hands, or with something they held in their hands, and opened the way to tennis, cricket, golf, croquet and many other games. Of these hitting games, tennis can probably produce one of the longest pedigrees.

'Real' or 'royal' tennis is, of course, a French game. It began as *'le jeu de paume'*. The ball was struck with the palm of the hand and was so hard that a glove was worn, as in fives, the name of which is supposed to come from the five fingers of the hand. Somebody discovered that he could give a swifter return by fitting strings across the palm of the glove. Then came a glove on a handle to provide more power. Then, a racket of strings with a wooden frame, or of parchment, for which purpose many valuable and historical records were destroyed.

Lord Aberdare* suggests that tennis was at first played not in palace out-buildings, but in monasteries, and the openings in the wall under the penthouse which surrounds a tennis court on three sides remind him of the sides of a cloister. He quotes writers from the twelfth century to show how popular the game was in ecclesiastical seminaries. Doubtless some bishops objected, but there is a record at St Brieuc of 'an ancient custom . . . on Easter day . . . of giving five tennis

* *The Story of Tennis* (Stanley Paul, London, 1959)

balls to the Bishop and three to each of the Canons and rackets with which to strike them'.

In time, the Church decided that tennis was not a game for priests, and forbad them to play it. The ban does not seem to have been very effective, for it had to be repeated in 1485, 1512 and 1693. Meanwhile it had become a game for kings and aristocrats. In the sixteenth century there were some two hundred and fifty courts in Paris alone. But Louis XVI was not a player and, without the king's support, the game lost its appeal. By the outbreak of the Revolution, there were only fifty-four courts in the whole of France.

The first royal player seems to have been Louis X, who ruled for only ten years. Tennis killed him—he drank too much cold water and sat for too long in a cool grotto after playing a game of tennis at Vincennes. Charles V, whose father had been captured by the English at Poitiers, was a keen player, and it was during his reign that betting became outrageously high. On one occasion, the Duke of Burgundy bet—and lost—his doublet, which was the nearest one could come in those days to putting one's shirt on a wager. (Much later, in a court built for Louis XV at Compiègne, a special niche for one's stakes was made just below the net cord.) Charles VI was the mad king, but a balcony, closed in by iron bars, was built outside his room in his castle at Creil-sur-Oise so that he could watch the tennis. Charles VIII, whose military adventures took him as far south as Naples, was barely taller than a dwarf; nevertheless, he cracked his skull against the lintel of a door in the Château d'Amboise as he was hurrying out to watch a tennis match. Francis I was so keen a player that he had a tennis court built on one of his ships—an unexpected prelude to the deck tennis of our day. Henry II played at the Louvre, 'dressed in white, wearing a doublet and a straw hat'. 'There is no formality.' wrote a contemporary, 'except that the net is lifted when he wishes to go under it.'

Despite his keenness, Charles V decreed that tennis must not be played by 'the lower classes'. Similar decrees were issued by several kings of England. In 1365, for example, Edward III decreed that his male subjects, during their hours of leisure, should 'use bows and arrows or pellets or bolts, and shall learn and practise the art of shooting, forbidding them under pain of imprisonment to meddle in hurling of stones, loggats and coits, hand-ball, football, club-ball, cambuca [a game played with a ball and a crooked stick; one of the ancestors of hockey], cock-fighting and other vain games of no value'. The frequent wars between England and France made such decrees necessary – the need for them became much less urgent of course, when the use of gunpowder made the archer archaic.

Such decrees, however, were not very effective. We find them repeated by monarch after monarch, even though they themselves were enthusiastic players. In the fifteenth century, the Ironmonger's Company – which, rather strangely, was the manufacturer of tennis balls – appealed to the king to forbid the import from France of 'tenys balles'. In 1571, Charles IX of France authorised a guild of tennis players and racket makers, with a coat of arms showing a racket surrounded by four balls, since tennis was now looked upon as 'one of the most honourable, worthy and healthy exercises which princes, peers, gentlemen and other distinguished persons can undertake'. Nor was the game as socially exclusive as it sounds; in 1590, Henry IV of France took part in a tennis match against the bakers of the town of Nantes. They were tactless enough to win the match (and the king's cash) and to refuse to give him his revenge, since they had played the maximum of three sets. The king's reaction was swift and effective – the next

3(a) Roman 'bread and circuses': gladiatorial combat (p. 13)

3(b) Peruvian Indians playing shuttlecock (p. 37)

4 Knuckle-bones, the forerunner of dice, as played
at Pompeii

day he issued a decree lowering the price of bread, and the bakers came hurrying back to make amends for their victory.

In 1601, this same Henry wrote a note to his wife which strongly resembles the letters received by thousands of golf widows in our own time. 'Enough of writing; I am off to play tennis. I kiss you a thousand times.' A year or two previously an Englishman, Sir Robert Dallington, had complained that the French were very immoderate in their exercises, 'especially in those that are somewhat violent; for ye may remember ye have seene them play Sets at Tennis in the heat of Summer, and height of the day, when others were scarce able to stirre out of dores. . . . And of this I dare assure you, that of this sort of pore people, there be more Tennis Players in France than Ale-drinkers, or Malt-wormes (as they call them) with us.'

Lord Aberdare quotes the following from a French treatise on tennis and rheumatism, written near the end of the eighteenth century; players 'make a broad belt with a napkin, which they tighten sufficiently by two knots on the kidneys. . . . This binding keeps the body firmer, strengthens the guts, upholds the liver against the frequent thrusts and shakes of the players, and prevents it from pulling back the diaphragm by its weight, which would make for difficulty in breathing.'

Tennis seems to have reached England in the thirteenth century, and there is an indication of its popularity, at least among the wealthy classes, in Shakespeare's *Henry V*. The king, it will be remembered, received a present of tennis balls from the Dauphin of France, and declared in reply:

When we have match'd our rackets to these balls
We will, in France, by God's grace, play a set
Shall strike his father's crown into the hazard . . .

Henry VIII was a very keen tennis player and, in 1532, accompanied by his pro, he went over to play in Calais. Having received Hampton Court as a 'gift' from Cardinal Wolsey—one of that unwise and unfortunate prelate's efforts to retain the royal favour—Henry had a court built there which is the oldest in the world still to be in use. He had four courts in the Palace of Westminster, two covered and two open. He was a great gambler as well as a great player, and he 'was moch entysed to playe at tennes and dice, which appetite, certayn craftie persones about hym perceyuynge, brought in Frenchmen and Lombardes, to make wagers with hym, and so he lost moch money'.

Ordinary people, meanwhile, were fined if they played tennis except 'during the twelve days of Christmas'. They might then play, but only in the presence of their employers. Noblemen and others with an income of over £100 were allowed to build courts in their grounds. Elizabeth was not a player, but an interested spectator, whose enthusiasm may have been reduced during a match between the Duke of Norfolk and the Earl of Leicester. The latter, we are told, 'being verie hotte and swetinge took the Queen's napken owte of her hande and wyped his face'. The Duke protested that the Earl was 'too sawcie'. What form the Queen's protest took is not, as far as I know, recorded.

The Stuarts were both great players and great gamblers. Cromwell, as one might surmise, did his best to forbid tennis, by that time an excuse for the most extravagant betting. Charles II continued to play after the Restoration, and Pepys writes in his diary for January 4th, 1664: 'To see how the king's play was extolled, without any cause at all, was a loathsome sight, though sometimes, indeed, he did play very well, and deserved to be commended; but such open flattery is beastly.' On one occasion, Charles had himself weighed before and after a day's tennis, and Pepys records that he lost four and a half pounds.

As a fashionable game, tennis went out with the Stuarts, although Frederick, Prince of Wales, managed to revive some interest in it in the middle of the eighteenth century. He died young, and the doctors decided that the cause of his death was a blow from a tennis ball— even though it had contained none of the forbidden materials I mentioned in my first chapter. Despite his many interests, he was not much beloved, and it is recorded that when his death was announced to his father, George II, the king, who was playing cards, did no more than comment '*Il est mort*'.

During some repairs to the roof of Westminster Hall, the workmen found a couple of tennis balls in the rafters. They had a solid core, wrapped round with human hair and sewn into a leather cover. More recently, 'real' tennis balls have been made of stitched material very tightly stuffed with rags. From time to time, of course, they need re-covering, but the original core is always retained, and some that were recently sent to Slazenger's to be re-covered were found to contain rags of uniforms dating back to the Crimean War. Several manufacturers are now making experimentally balls of solid rubber, covered with the same cloth as is used for lawn tennis balls.

The theory that tennis was originally played in cloisters seems to be strengthened by the fact that for a long time the size of the court was not standardised. A court nowadays is fixed at 96 feet in length and nearly 32 feet in width (as against the 78 feet and 36 feet of a doubles court in lawn tennis). The net is five feet high at the sides and three feet at the centre. The so-called penthouse, a little more than seven feet high at its lower edge, runs along the two ends of the court and one side of it. At the service end is the *dedans*, a rectangular hole in the back wall; at the far end there is a small square opening, the *grille*. Beneath the penthouse along the side of the court are the galleries, and a ball hit so that it goes into the *dedans*, the *grille* or the last gallery on the far side of the net scores a point. Since this is not a book which aims at telling people how the different games are played, I can leave the very complicated subject of scoring at 'real' tennis. For which I am sincerely thankful.

The game now has so few devotees that one does not easily realise how popular, or rather how fashionable, it once was. The kings of Spain were playing tennis as far back as the thirteenth century. Florence–a great city for guilds–had a guild of tennis ball and racket makers in 1550. The first reference to the game in North America seems to have been in 1659, when Peter Stuyvesant, Governor of New York, decreed that tennis and a number of other games must not be played on October 15th, which was a day of Universal Fasting and Prayer. In the German-speaking countries of Europe, a tennis court was called a Ballplatz, and it appears that the former Austrian Foreign Office, referred to by generations of historians as the Ballhausplatz, was built on or near the site of a tennis court during the reign of Ludwig XIV. It is not, as I had always thought, on or near the site of a ballroom in which officers in splendiferous uniforms led their beautiful partners in the exhilaration of a Viennese waltz. A pity!

*   *   *

Several people claimed to have invented lawn tennis. There is a reference to 'field tennis' in the *Sporting Magazine* in 1793–the writer forecast that 'field tennis threatens ere long to bowl out cricket'. But most of the credit undoubtedly goes to a British major, Walter Wingfield, who took out a patent in 1874 granting him the monopoly of equipment for a game which might easily have been strangled at birth by the name he gave it–Sphairistike. This, he explained, had been the name given by the ancient Greeks to a similar game. Lawn tennis, he said, had the advantage over 'real' tennis that 'it may be played in any weather by people of any age and both sexes. In a hard frost the nets may be erected on the ice, and the players equipped with skates; the game assumes a new feature, and gives an opening for the exhibition of much grace and science.'

The Major, then, was a pioneer towards whom we must feel grateful. But perhaps a little lacking in humour? Or am I prejudiced because he thought so poorly of that most graceful and strenuous of games, badminton? He dismissed it as 'simply Battledore and Shuttlecock over a string, and not suitable for out of doors'. Even his last six words are not quite correct, for most badminton champions come from South-east Asia, and have learnt how to play badminton in odd clearings between the attap huts and the coconut palms. Badminton and lawn tennis were invented at about the same time, and the most widely accepted version of badminton's beginning is that a group of guests at Badminton, the Gloucestershire home of the Duke of Beaufort, borrowed battledores and shuttlecocks from the nursery one wet afternoon and played in the great hall. But it would be as absurd to compare that beginning with championship badminton of today as to compare snap with canasta.

Shuttlecocks in one form or another have been used all over the world; their discovery became inevitable almost as soon as men learnt to use their hands. North American Indians made them out of maize husks tied into a small, tight bundle into which they stuck two or three feathers. But they used only their hands instead of rackets, and their game consisted of seeing how many

37

times the shuttlecock could be hit into the air. This game, or occupation, seems to have preceded the arrival in North America of the Spaniards. Chinese children make their shuttlecocks of a bunch of feathers fastened to a coin, their coins being conveniently made with a hole in the middle so that people with no pockets can thread their cash on a string and wear it in safety as a necklace.

If the Badminton House theory is correct, it provides one more instance of a children's game adapted and improved by adults for their own amusement. Another game which probably developed in this way is table tennis, or, early in the present century, ping-pong. When I was a very small boy, my parents used to organise ping-pong parties; they certainly did not then foresee the day when some eight thousand clubs would be affiliated to the British Table Tennis Association, member of a Federation of some seventy nations. In those days, any table would do, provided it were about five and a half feet long and four feet wide. (Now the official measurements are nine feet by five and a half.) We had a long, celluloid cylinder with three small teeth at one end of it; by pressing the cylinder down on the ball so that it passed these teeth, the ladies could pick it up without the discomfort of stooping down in their tight-laced corsets. (Similar contraptions, of course, exist in many golf clubs for the collection of balls driven off a practice tee.) The evenings ended (as I well remember, since I used to creep downstairs in my nightshirt to taste the trifle laced with sherry) with a buffet supper. Nor were such evenings as insipid as they may sound, for my parents were tough athletes, with my father playing hockey for his county at the age of forty and my mother playing in small and easy-going tennis tournaments at south coast resorts. For amateurs, those were the days! But now, with players standing yards back from the table and putting a screw on the ball that would have been condemned as most unsporting sixty years ago, table tennis has become as different from ping-pong as badminton from battledore and shuttlecock.

*   *   *

Why the name 'tennis'? Why 'deuce'? Why 'love'? There are several explanations of the names, some of which are highly unconvincing. One, for example, is that, at one stage of its evolution, tennis was known in France as *la longue paume*—the *jeu de paume*, or hand-ball, being extended by a racket—and ten players, five a side, were involved in this game. Ten players? Then call the game 'tennis'. But why the English 'ten' should be brought into the name of a French game nobody seems to know. The much more probable explanation is that the name comes from '*Tenez*', or 'Play', which was called out before the ball was served in 'real' tennis, and, later, in lawn tennis. I have seen no satisfactory explanation of 'Love', but 'Deuce' is easier—apparently, when one player scored forty (or forty-five, as it was for a time) the scorer called out '*à un*', signifying that one point was needed for game. If both players scored forty, he called '*à deux*', since two consecutive points had to be won. And '*à deux*', in the course of time, became 'deuce'.

A few lines about Wimbledon. In 1868, three enthusiastic croquet players, Henry Jones, his cousin, Whitmore Jones, and J. W. Walsh, the editor of the *Field*, decided to found an All-England Croquet Club. They appointed one of the reporters of the *Field* to look for a suitable ground and, with two other friends, each subscribed a sovereign to pay his expenses. Negotiations with Prince's Club in Hans Place, with the Royal Toxophilites in Regent's Park, and with the Crystal Palace all came to nothing. More than a year went by before an offer came of four acres at Wimbledon for an annual rent of £50, and the All-England Croquet Club came into existence. It held its first championship meeting in 1870. A notice on the board requested gentlemen not to play in their shirtsleeves when ladies were present.

John Cliff* describes how, five years later, Henry Jones persuaded his fellow-members to use part of the club grounds for two new games—badminton and lawn tennis, and in 1877 the name was changed to All-England Croquet and Lawn Tennis Club. Six years later croquet disappeared from the club's title, but it reappeared in second place after another twenty years had elapsed—Wimbledon had become the All-England Tennis and Croquet Club. A Ladies' Championship was inaugurated in 1884, and one proposal before the committee (which, however, rejected it) would have astonished the hardy, short-shorted female competitors of today—women players should be given five minutes rest between each set. I notice that, in a photograph of an international match between England and the United States in 1883, almost every male member of the spectators is wearing a top hat.

The present Wimbledon ground was bought shortly after the first world war. Much of the credit for the development of the game also goes to the M.C.C. at Lords, for it published standardised rules in 1875, and one of its most famous members—J. M. Heathcote, who was M.C.C. champion of 'real' tennis from 1867 to 1881—initiated the present tennis ball. Finding that the ordinary rubber ball was awkward to deal with on a wet court, he persuaded his wife to cover one with flannel; since when all tennis balls have been so covered. The size and weight of the tennis ball have slightly increased

* *The Romance of Wimbledon* (Hutchinson, London, 1949)

since his day. It must now be between $2\frac{37}{64}$ and $2\frac{43}{64}$ inches, and, when dropped from a height of one hundred inches, it should rebound between fifty-three and fifty-eight inches.

Lawn tennis very rapidly became popular in the United States. One pioneer of the game was a Dr James Dwight, who played at Nahant, near Boston, within a year of its invention in England. Another pioneer was a certain Miss Outerbridge, who brought equipment from the British garrison on Bermuda to her brother, who was a director of the Staten Island Cricket and Baseball Club. (Cricket and baseball in that order. Americans, please note.) In 1900, a Harvard student, Dwight F. Davis, offered the Davis Cup for championship competitions between his country and Great Britain. The first matches were held in that same year at Longwood, near Boston. The cup was won by the Americans. (Britons, please note.)

CHAPTER FOUR

From Pall Mall to the Cricket Pitch

Croquet and Pall Mall· Basketball· Baseball and rounders· Lacrosse·
Hockey and hiccoughs·History of cricket· A dangerous leveller

CROQUET, which was displaced at Wimbledon by lawn tennis, is another game with a long history. It has points of resemblance to the French game of *paille maille* or *pallemail*, which is commemorated in the names of Pall Mall and the Mall in London. It was being played in the south of France in the thirteenth century, but was at the height of its fashion in the seventeenth, when Madame de Sevigné referred to it as *'un aimable jeu pour les personnes bien faites et adroites'* – a description which will please those who play it, but may surprise some of those who only watch. In the Middle Ages, on Shrove Tuesday, the Bishop of Avranches, in Normandy, used to hit a ball through the streets with his mallet. Why, I do not know, but quite probably neither did he. (Nor do I know why Shrove Tuesday used to be a particular day for football in England.)

Pall mall was very popular with the Stuart kings. There seem to have been several varieties of it, but generally it was played on a course some four hundred yards long, at each end of which was a hoop, raised some ten feet above the ground. The ball, made of boxwood root, was about the size of a cricket ball, and the stick was shaped very like a croquet mallet (hence, it was said, the word 'mall') the face of which was cut at an angle, so that the player could 'lift' the ball, as a golfer does with a 'spoon'. This he needed to do, since he had to hit the ball through the hoops, which were called 'passes' or 'ports', in the lowest possible number of strokes. Thus the game had some resemblance to both golf and croquet, but also to the earliest form of billiards, which was played on level ground and in which the player, with a very rudimentary cue called a 'battoon', had to send his ball through a hoop stuck in the earth. From this 'rural billiards', came the present game, and in its earliest form the billiard table had an ivory 'port' or 'pass' fixed where the 'spot' now is.

Pall mall, with its hard ball, could be dangerous, and the mall was flanked on either side by a high fence, so that the player could not slice his ball into the rough. In his diary for May 15th, 1663, Pepys writes that he 'walked in the Park, discoursing with the keeper of the Pall Mall, who was sweeping of it; who told me that the earth is mixed that do floor the Mall, and that over all there is cockle-shells powdered and spread to keep it fast; which, however, in dry weather turns to dust and deads the ball'.

Something much more akin to present-day croquet reached England by way of Ireland, where it was first played on Lord Lonsdale's lawn in 1852 – the game had been introduced into Ireland by Huguenot refugees from France after the revocation of the Edict of Nantes. In the United States, croquet, with rather different rules, is called 'roque', being the French word for roquet – and, in case you do not play the game, roquet is the term used when your ball hits another, and croquet is the term used when you follow up a roquet by placing your ball against your victim's.

*　　*　　*

The history of basketball, now one of the most widely-played games in the world, is blessedly easy. It was invented in 1891 by a Y.M.C.A. gymnastic instructor, James Naismith, at Springfield, Massachusetts. The histories of two other games from the New

World, baseball and lacrosse, are more difficult to write about with confidence.

The slightly condescending belief of most Englishmen that baseball is merely a form of the old English children's game of rounders is, not surprisingly, rejected by most Americans, although rounders itself has a respectable ancestry, being about four hundred years old. In order to emphasise the Americanness of the American national game, a National Baseball Hall of Fame and Museum was opened in 1939 at Cooperstown, in the State of New York, to celebrate the centenary of the game, as designed by Abner Doubleday, later to become a general and a veteran of Gettysburg. In 1908, an impressive but somewhat biased 'committee of research' had reached the conclusion that the rules, and even the name, owed their existence to General Doubleday.

But the committee seems to have been suffering from xenophobia; there is ample evidence of the link between baseball and rounders (the rules of which were more recently altered in Britain also, to make it more suitable for adults). The *Encyclopaedia Britannica*–despite its name, edited and published in the United States–makes nonsense of the claims put forward on behalf of the gallant general. The game of rounders was being played in the States well before 1839. So was a game called 'old cat'–the 'cat' being the short piece of wood used in the very ancient game of tipcat. It is about six inches in length and two inches in diameter. The ends are tapered, so that, when the cat is placed on the ground and hit at either end with a club, it jumps into the air, and the wielder of the club takes a terrific swipe at it. The batter in old cat then runs from base to base, as in rounders–or, for that matter, in baseball. One old cat was played by three or more players. In two old cat, three old cat or four old cat the number of players might be increased to fourteen or more. (Chinese children also play a game in which a boy with a club stands in a six-foot square and has to hit a cat very similar to that used in tipcat). Unless the cat is shaped with great care, its leap into the air will be very erratic. Henry Moore was a keen player when he was a boy in the North of England and Sir Herbert Read* suggests that his shaping of the cat, or 'piggy' as it was called, 'was perhaps Henry's earliest experience of a sculptural sensation'.

But the claim for Cooperstown is not destroyed merely by the fact that rounders and old cat, with their strong similarities to baseball, were being played in America before 1839. More important is the fact that other writers described the game of baseball—and even called it by that name—before that year. *The Little Pretty Pocket-book*, published in England in 1744 and in America in 1762, had a description and a woodcut of the game. An American writer, Thurlow Weed—please believe that I am not inventing these names—wrote about a baseball club that had been founded in about 1825. A much more famous American writer, Oliver Wendell Holmes, once told an interviewer that he had played a lot of baseball at Harvard in 1829. And there is other evidence that General Doubleday, at most, merely altered or codified the rules of an already well-established game. So Americans who are depressed by the links between their national game and the English children's game of rounders may take consolation in the fact that baseball is an older game than visitors to the Cooperstown museum would lead them to believe.

Furthermore, of course, the development from rounders, as played by children with their school caps or their jackets to mark each base, and baseball, as played by Babe Ruth and his distinguished successors, has been as great as that between the first tennis matches at

* *Henry Moore* by Herbert Read (Thames & Hudson, London, 1965)

Wimbledon and those in a contemporary Davis Cup final. In rounders, the ball was soft and might be hit in any direction; in baseball, the ball is hard and must be hit inside an arc of ninety degrees—if it goes more to the right or the left, it falls on 'foul ground' and does not permit the batter to run to first base.

Several attempts have been made to arouse English interest in baseball and to re-arouse American interest in cricket. National prejudice, however, has proved too strong. Baseball is achieving great popularity in parts of Asia, and was well-established in Japan before the arrival of American troops in that country after the last war. On the other hand, one finds a touching loyalty to cricket even in those parts of the former British Commonwealth where nationalism is passing through its inevitable anti-British phase. My chief recollection of a three-hour visit to the former colony of The Gambia is of the way in which the important official buildings of Bathurst, the pleasant little capital, are grouped, not round some pompous palace, but round the cricket field.

*   *   *

Lacrosse, the national ball game of Canada, is said to derive its name from the curved, netted stick with which it is played, and which looks like a bishop's crozier, or *crosse* in French. This game, at least, is not a foreign importation; it has been developed from a game invented by the original Indian inhabitants, who played it on a very large scale—there might be a thousand men on either side and the goals might be as much as half a mile apart. The teams generally belonged to different tribes and their games were preceded by solemn dances. The players were stimulated to greater efforts by their wives, who beat them with canes. The game, excluding this activity by the wives, was taken up with enthusiasm by the French Canadians, but it was adopted as the national game only in 1867, when the country became a British Dominion.

Hockey, like lacrosse, is too often treated with disparagement, as a game more suitable for women than for men. Strange, since a hockey ball is very hard, a hockey stick is more likely to do damage than a cricket bat, and my friend John Betjeman is not the first man to have noticed how tough, muscular and alarming a hockey girl may become. Hockey can claim to be a very ancient game indeed. Since the very earliest days, people have used sticks to hit stones, pieces of wood, or anything else that could be made to travel a satisfying distance. Within a few centuries they must have begun to invent rules, which developed into such games as hockey, golf, cricket and tennis. The need for such activities was recognised by, among many others, a certain Dr Andrew Boorde who wrote a *Dyetery of Helth* in 1542. 'Before you go to your refection', he wrote, 'moderately exercise your body with some labour, or playing at the tennis, or casting a bowl, or poising weights or plummets of lead in your hands, or some other thing to open your pores and to augment natural heat.'

The word 'hockey' is believed to derive from *'hoquet'*, meaning a 'hooked stick' in old French (but 'hiccoughs' in the French of today). In one form or another, however, the game is older even than the French language itself, for the ancient Romans played a game called *paganica*, with curved sticks and balls covered with leather—obviously an ancestor of hockey and probably also of golf. In Ireland, under the name of 'hurling', with a slightly different stick and slightly different rules, it can be traced back for at least a thousand years. There were two varieties—'hurling to goals' and 'hurling to the country'. In the latter game the goals might be three or four miles apart, and R. Carew, in his

Survey of Cornwall, published in 1602, wrote that 'you shall sometimes see twenty or thirty lie together in the water, scrambling and scratching for the ball', which was made of some very light wood. It could be carried or thrown; it must not be kicked. Another indication of the game's age is contained in *English Mediaeval Pilgrimage*.* There it is written of St Clement the Northumbrian seventh-century bishop of Lindisfarne, that 'it was while he was playing hockey in which he excelled that he had his first revelation'.

*   *   *

I must now turn to a game which I hated because I played it so badly and loved because I so enjoyed watching other people play it. That morning at Bournemouth more than sixty years ago, when I collected the autographs of both W. G. Grace and C. B. Fry, remains as vividly in my mind as does the day when I unexpectedly won a parliamentary election. Or that day when I saw my first white rhinoceros walking with such majesty in the Hluhluwe National Park in Zululand. Or that night during the war when our 'tug' left us high above Salisbury Plain and our glider hovered for a few minutes in that great, starlit silence before my companion set about the task of bringing us down safely to the black land below. Trumper and 'Ranji', G. L. Jessop, 'Plum' Warner, C. P. Mead and that splendidly erratic and lovable batsman, Sammy Woods—what players they were! And how easily I could become sentimental about that damned game!

The origin of cricket? Dr Johnson defined it as 'a sport in which the contenders drive a ball with sticks in opposition to each other'. Thus defined, it might have been one of half-a-dozen earlier games, such as stool-ball, club-ball, hand-in-or-hand-out, or cat-and-dog. In stool-

* By D. J. Hall (Routledge & Kegan Paul, London, 1965)

5(a) 'Royal' tennis (p. 35)

5(b) Indians playing 'La Crosse' (p. 46)

6(b) The beginning of baseball (p. 45)

vaches garter ne porra mes entendre

6(c) Nuns and monks playing cricket? (p. 50)

6(a) Pall mall, game of the Stuart kings (p. 43)

ball, played in the north of England, the batsman stood in front of a milking stool and—according to some authorities—defended this wicket with his hand. This, however, can scarcely be correct, for J. Aubrey, in *The Natural History of Wiltshire*, published in 1671, wrote that 'a stobbal ball is about four inches in diameter and as hard as a stone'. There must, therefore, have been a bat of some kind. In club-ball, a straight bat was used, but there was no wicket. So cricket would seem to be a compromise between these two games, but it also has some resemblance to hand-in-or-hand-out, to which I refer later. In cat-and-dog, the 'dog' was the bat or club, and the 'cat' was very similar to the 'cat' in tipcat; the man with the dog had to keep the cat out of a hole in the ground. This game, much more complicated than I have made it sound, was played by Bunyan amongst others.

The great French encyclopaedia, Larousse, claims that 'cricket is only a modification of the game called in France *"crosse"* or *"criquet"*'. No Englishman will be prepared to accept that, and still less so when he reflects that, as I have already pointed out, one translation of *'crosse'* is a bishop's crozier, or a curved stick resembling one. But in fact early cricket bats were curved, and an Anglo-French dictionary published in 1611 translates *'crosse'* as 'crozier or bishop's staffe, also a cricket staffe, or the crooked staffe wherewith boys play at cricket'. Andrew Lang, in the Badminton Library book on cricket, wrote that the *'crosse'* was also the club 'used in French Flanders at the local kind of golf'.

The most widely-accepted origin of the name in Britain seems to be that it comes from an Anglo-Saxon word, 'cricc', meaning a shepherd's staff, and that the earliest players were shepherds on the South Downs, using their crooks as bats. I wonder whether by any chance the English may be suffering a little from the same kind of xenophobia as affected the Americans when they founded the Cooperstown Baseball Museum.

The first known drawing of cricket dates from the middle of the thirteenth century, and it shows a man holding his bat upright, handle down, more in the stance of a baseball player than that of a cricketer. The Bodleian Library has a drawing, dated April 1344, in which the batsman, bowler and fielders are all monks or nuns (and I have already recorded the suggestion that the first games of tennis may have been played by monks in their cloisters). Here again, the batsman has his bat held upright, but in his left hand. The bat is slightly curved, and it was not until about 1770 that bats became straight.

In common with golf, but unlike most other ball games, cricket began as a countryman's game, and I have often watched matches at the pleasant little Hampshire village of Hambledon in the belief that this is where the first games of cricket had been played. But it all depends upon what you call cricket. Hambledon became famous only in the eighteenth century; some three hundred years earlier there was a game involving batsmen, bowlers and fielders, which was called 'Hondyn or Handoute' (hand-in-or-hand-out). This was included in the list of games forbidden by a series of English kings because they interfered with the practice of archery. They did not then realise that it would later be claimed that one of the greatest British battles was won on the playing fields of a school called Eton.

The wicket, in the days of Hambledon's glory, was 'two stumps with a stump laid across', and these stumps were at least as wide apart as they were high. Bowling was underhand, and along the ground. In one Hambledon match in 1775 – Hambledon versus All England – the club's most famous bowler, Edward Stevens, better known as 'Lumpy', bowled three times between the stumps without knocking off the bail, and shortly afterwards the wicket was made larger and a third stump was added. The width of the bat was limited to $4\frac{1}{4}$ inches after one player had produced a bat as wide as the stumps, and one of the rules added after 1780 was to the effect that a fielder might not stop a ball with his hat. The first batsmen to wear pads were so scoffed at by the onlookers that they found it advisable to take them off again.

The first reference to cricket by name seems to have been in 1593, in the course of an enquiry about a piece of land at Guildford, wrongfully enclosed by a local innkeeper. According to Russell's *History of Guildford*, one of the witnesses stated that 'when he was a scholler in the free school of Guildford' (more than forty years previously) 'he and several of his fellowes did runne and play there at crickett and other plaies'. The Rev. Thomas Wilson, writing in the first half of the seventeenth century, complained that Maidstone had formerly been 'a very prophane town in as much as I have seen morrice-dancing, cudgel-playing, stool-ball, crickets and many other sports openly and publicly indulged in on the Lord's Day'.

The reverend gentleman had some cause for complaint, for most of these activities—though not, I imagine morris dancing—provided excuses for a terrific amount of betting, and, although it lessened considerably after the Stuarts, the *Evening Post* of August 7th, 1729 described cricket a match between two teams, one from London and one from Dartford, 'for a considerable sum of money wages and Betts and the latter beat the former very much'. In 1735, the Prince of Wales—Prince Frederick, whose death was attributed to a blow either by a cricket ball or, as mentioned in the previous chapter, by a tennis ball—and Lord Middlesex promoted two matches for a thousand pounds.

The first 'county' match was played between London and Kent in 1719. In 1744, Kent played against All England on the Artillery Ground, Finsbury. And in 1787 the Marylebone Cricket Club was founded. Some of its members had belonged to the Artillery Ground Club, mentioned above. They moved, first, to the White Conduit Club, and then to Lord's. But not to the Lord's of today. Thomas Lord, whose family had been compelled to leave Scotland after the '45 Rebellion, had laid out a ground where Dorset Square now stands. In 1811, he moved–taking the turf with him–to a ground near the present Regent's Canal. The cutting of the canal made yet another move necessary. Lord, always with his precious turf, went to the present ground in St John's Wood.

Since 1788, the M.C.C. has been the accepted authority on all matters concerning cricket. Or on almost all– the Australians have on occasions taken the initiative in making small alterations to the rules. Incidentally, no less an authority than Anthony Trollope wrote this in 1868: 'our own dependencies in India cannot create native players; and although, by unremitting diligence– more for the pleasure of overcoming difficulties than anything else–one or two Englishmen have taught the Australian native to present a more than creditable appearance, their existence is a mere phenomenon which has no significance so far as the nationality of the game is concerned.' Just ten years after he had written this article in *British Sports and Pastimes*, an Australian team visited England and defeated a good M.C.C. team by nine wickets.

Rather surprisingly, cricket was being played in the United States some two centuries ago, and the chief match of the year, between the United States and Canada, preceded the first matches between England and Australia by more than thirty years. Very probably, as the non-British percentage of Americans increased, cricket would anyhow have lost ground, but the decay was greatly hastened by the American Civil War, which made it impossible for would-be players to import equipment from England.

Efforts to popularise cricket on the European continent have failed, although there are rather pathetic clubs here and there, to remind imperialists of past glories. The game is still played on Corfu, for example, and I read recently of a match between the Brussels British Cricket Club and a scratch team of British journalists accredited to the European Community. A certain Henry Matthews, in his *Diary of an Invalid*, described a cricket match in Naples very shortly after the Battle of Waterloo. Eton defeated 'the World'.

Near most villages there is a fairly level field available for cricket, with sheep or cattle to keep the grass under some sort of control. Not so near towns, especially after the Industrial Revolution and the Land Enclosure Acts had combined to rob the people of their open spaces. It is only fairly recently that large firms have had the foresight to realise the financial value of healthy workers, and have spent large sums on sports grounds in the suburbs. Some of the greatest cricketers of Victorian times–Tom Emmett, for example, who was born in 1841–had to learn their cricket in the streets or on the turnpike roads. But cricket was for a long time a rural game, and one of very little social importance–if it was played by the sons of the gentry at their schools, it was abandoned by them when they grew up. Betting, which has ruined so many games, may be said to have saved cricket. How and why?

I have already called attention to the great amount of betting that went on under the Stuarts. Things changed very drastically during the stringent days of the Commonwealth, whose enemies found it advisable to retire to their country estates where, to cheat boredom, many of them took part in village cricket. They became patrons of their village teams. They reinforced these village teams by enlisting the more athletic and energetic of their friends. They arranged matches with other villages, and thus found new excuses for betting. Village cricket became, and has remained, one of the most typical features of English rural life. In 1748, the legal authorities decided that cricket was 'a very manly game, not bad in itself, but only in the ill-use made of it by betting more than ten pounds on it, but that is bad and against the law'. There was also a good deal of drinking, the licensing laws being less eccentric in previous centuries than they are now, and it being then 'very manly' to drink oneself under the dinner table. In the *Leicester Journal* of July 29th, 1836, a wish was expressed that, 'for the sake of the game, the players would keep back the convivial part until the stumps be drawn, the bowling etc. on Wednesday betraying symptoms of weakness'.

With continuing patronage of 'the county', cricket became more and more respectable. Women cricketers are less of a novelty than is generally supposed. There is a record of a women's cricket match played in Surrey in 1778, and it is claimed that the first round-arm bowler was a woman. The mother of Dr W. G. Grace was a keen player. A circular about one women's club, issued in 1892, stated that 'every effort is made to keep the organisation in every respect select and refined. . . . A matron accompanies each eleven to all engagements.' By the beginning of the present century, cricket carried with it more social status than any other outdoor activity except, perhaps, riding to hounds. On the scorecards of county matches which I collected when I was a boy, there were far more 'gentlemen'—identifiable by the printing of their initials as well as their surnames—

than 'players', or professionals. The 'gentlemen' came proudly down the main steps of the pavilion; the 'players' came out of a gate at the side. Nevertheless, it has always been a game in which class barriers were less real than in most other games. In 1746, in a match between Kent and All-England, Lord John Sackville played under the captaincy of his own head gardener. Three years previously, *The Gentlemen's Magazine* had complained that 'great and little people, baronets and butchers, went out to field together'. Cricket, complained the article, was 'a dangerous leveller'. A more serious complaint in the same article was that 'it propagates a spirit of idleness at the very time when, with the utmost industry, our debts, taxes and decay of trade will scarcely allow us to get bread'. It is comforting to be reminded that there were idlers, debts and economic crises well over two centuries ago.

CHAPTER FIVE

Child's Play

The war game · Children's games and fertility rites · The May-pole · London street games · Hoops, tops and stilts · Games in Greece and Rome — The Olympic Games

FROM the point of view of history, the games of children are more interesting than those of the adults whom they so frequently copy and sometimes caricature. Girls copy their mothers and dress up their dolls. Boys copy their fathers and run round the house shouting 'bang! bang!' at each other—their fathers, it is true, probably dress in drab civilian clothes and go off each morning to the office or the factory, but most of them cannot fail to be aware that they are heroes to their sons only when they can boast about their adventures in war-time. Boys—and quite a lot of adults—are irresistibly attracted by uniforms, and Huizinga* reminds us how persistent and deep-rooted—even after two world wars—is the idea of war as a game, with rules as strict as those of any children's game.

The age of chivalry, for example, was an age when rules were respected in the belief that war was a God-ordained method of deciding on which side were right and justice. After all, it is not so very long since a suspect was judged innocent or guilty by the state of his arm after he had plunged it into boiling water. Another test was to compel an accused person to grasp a piece of red-hot metal; if his hand did not fester after three days, the poor devil was declared innocent. 'Ordeal by battle' remained theoretically legal in Britain until 1818; even

* *Homo Ludens* by J. Huizinga (Routledge & Kegan Paul, London, 1949)

today some Frenchmen hold that a wrong can be righted by a duel. In the Middle Ages, there were all kinds of chivalrous preludes to battle, so that its result should be more obviously the judgment of God, and Huizinga mentions the case of Henry of Trastanara who, in 1367, gave up his extremely favourable terrain at Najera, in Spain, in order to meet his opponent in the open field. (His chivalrous behaviour but poor tactics ended in his defeat.)

Only now, when the rules of the game have been flouted by deliberate defiance of international obligations and the appalling involvement of civilians—the spectators, as it were—is this form of contest robbed of its romantic and game-like features and shown up as a suicidal and bestial struggle for power. But one dare not anticipate that small boys will soon replace their toy bombers by toy computers or their toy soldiers by toy scientists; they are very conservative, and so many of their games have names that go far back into history, that they may still be playing with toy guns and bombers after adults have come to their senses about war.

There is one Irish game, very similar to 'I'm the king of the castle' (in itself rather out-dated), which is called 'The walls of Troy'. An English game similar to 'Cowboys and Indians' is called 'Roman soldiers'. The London Bridge that has fallen down was not destroyed— as many people imagine—by the Great Fire of 1666; it was built in 994 and was destroyed some twenty years later by Olaf, king and patron saint of Norway and ally of Ethelred the Unready, in a war against the Danes. Olaf's men tied ropes round the pillars of the bridge and rowed hard in an attempt to pull it down; this, however, failed, so he had his boats moored across the river from one pier to another, and let the ebbing tide do most of the work of destruction. (The first stone bridge was finished in 1209, and was paid for principally by a tax on wool, which gave rise to the legend that its pillars rested, quite literally, on wool-packs.)

There are songs or games about falling bridges in several countries, and Henry Bett* suggests that these references were almost certainly linked to the pagan custom of immuring a living sacrifice in the foundations of a building or a bridge in order to appease the spirits. He recalls the legend that two Romans, Quintillius and Faustulus, were buried under a huge stone when Romulus founded Rome.

Probably most children who halt a game by calling *'pax'* no longer realise that they are speaking in Latin, or that, when they cross their fingers, they are making the sign of the cross. In the game variously known as 'touch', 'tag' or 'tig', and in other games as well, one achieves safety by touching iron, and apparently 'he' or the pursuer, is often called 'Horney'. But why should iron give one safety from the devil? Northern Europeans ward off misfortune by touching wood; Italians do so by touching iron. I had always believed the wood was supposed to represent the True Cross and the iron to represent its nails. (It was one of these alleged nails that, beaten out into a very fine circle and fastened inside the Iron Crown of Lombardy, gave that item of regalia its immense symbolic importance.) But several authorities attribute a pre-Christian mystical value to metals. Iron or, even more, bronze or brass were supposed to have the power to save the pursued from his pursuer. One can imagine the effect on primitive, stone-age people of their first experience of a meteorite! Well might they attribute divine power to the iron and other minerals that composed it.

Any number of children's games seem to be derived from fertility rites. 'Nuts in May'—the 'nuts' should be

* *The Games of Children* (Methuen, London, 1929)

'knots', or small bunches of flowers—and 'I sent a letter to my love' are only two of several ring games of this kind. Ring games, says Daiken,* represent the winning of a wife; games in two opposing lines are obviously based on the idea of conflict. It is believed that early Christian objections to dancing had less to do with the sexual desires to which it might give rise than to its former connection with pagan beliefs, since dancing nearly always played a great part in pagan rites. Greeks and Romans danced and jumped to stimulate the growth of their crops (so, too, do the participants in the Furry Dance in Cornwall's town of Helston each year on May 8th, although few of them are aware of the part they are playing in encouraging a good harvest). In several countries, farmers used to leap as high as they could when they sowed their corn in order to stimulate its growth; probably several children's jumping and skipping games have a similar origin.

The most famous pagan celebration of the return of spring was, of course, linked with the May-pole, which was condemned during the Commonwealth as 'a heathenish vanity, generally abused to superstition and wickednesse'. I daresay the prevailing excitement led a good many couples to slip away into the undergrowth, but so does Carnival, and so would Christmas if it were not so damned cold at that time of year. May Day was certainly a more cheerful, and possibly a more Christian, occasion when young men and girls danced round the May-pole than it is now, when they march angrily through the streets carrying political banners.

Philip Stubbes, a Puritan writer in the sixteenth century who wrote an *Anatomie of Abuses*, deplored the importance given to the May-pole. 'Twentie or fortie yoke of oxen, everye Oxe havyng a sweete nosegaie of

* *Children's Games Throughout the Year* by Leslie Daiken (Batsford, London, 1949)

flowers tyed on the tippe of his hornes, and these Oxen drawe home this Maie-poole (this stinckyng Idoll rather) which is couered all over with Flowers and Hearbes, bounde rounde aboute with stringes, from the top to the bottom.' He also protested against the way in which people went off into the country 'where they spende all night in pastymes, and in the mornyng they returne, bringing with them birch bowes and branches of trees to deck their assemblies withall'. Poor Mr Stubbes! J. Strutt* has similar complaints to make about bonfires on Midsummer Eve, when people 'indulge themselves with filthy and unlawful games, to which they add glotony and drunkenness and the commission of many other shameful indecencies'.

After the restoration of the Stuarts, the cult of the May-pole was also restored. James II, when Duke of York, personally supervised the work of twelve sailors who erected a May-pole 134 feet high in the Strand in 1661. It stood there for fifty-six years. When it was dismantled, part of it was used by Sir Isaac Newton to support a new telescope that had been presented by a French astronomer to the Royal Society.

Blind man's buff is one of the games which has become more gentle with the passing of the centuries and with its limitation to children. Its English name comes from the old French 'buffe'—a buffet or a blow. The victim was blindfolded, and then slapped by the other players until he managed to catch one and to guess his identity. The blows were often violent. Hoodman blind and hot cockles were variants of blindman's buff. This game may have been in the minds of the men who seized Jesus before the Crucifixion, and of whom St Luke wrote: 'And when they had blindfolded him, they struck him on the face, and asked him, saying, "Prophesy,

* *Sports and Pastimes of the People of England* (Tegg, London, 1838)

who is it that smote thee?".' The game was certainly
known during the period of the Roman Empire, and
Pollux, tutor to the Emperor Commodus, less than two
centuries after the death of Christ, wrote a description
of it, calling it the game of the brass fly.

Blind man's buff to the French and the Belgians is
called *colin-maillard*, in memory of a famous warrior
from Liège, knighted in 999 by Robert the Pious, King
of France. He had been blinded during a battle against
the Count of Louvain, but he continued his career as a
soldier with such success that, after his death, the king
introduced in military tournaments an event in which a
blindfolded knight fought a group of other knights with
blunted weapons. Those of us who deplore the amount
of cruelty in the world today may derive a little consolation from the fact that, little more than a century ago, a
favourite form of blind man's buff in the Pyrenees consisted in blindfolding a young man, turning him round
several times until he was giddy, and then giving him a
sabre with which he had to try to cut off the head of a
duck hanging in front of him. If he succeeded, the duck,
or what remained of the poor beast, was his.

*　　*　　*

Nothing about children's games seems to me more
fascinating than the ingenuity which children themselves put into them. In a book on London street games,
written most unexpectedly by Norman Douglas and
published a year after his *Old Calabria* and a year before
his *South Wind*, there is a formidable list of games
played by children with the help of caps, stones, sticks
or nothing at all. The list is also a useful reminder that
most games invented by children emphasise their
desire to grow up, whereas many games invented by
adults clearly are intended above all to keep the children
quiet and out of mischief.

The names of several London games listed by Norman Douglas have historical origins. Among them are King Caesar, King of the Barbary, Queen Anne, King John says no, green man rise-O, hiding hats in the Houses of Parliament, high treason, we are Romans, and Chinese orders. Other games seem to have no historical connections, but their names are so intriguing that they really deserve wider publicity. Sally round the jampot, hat under the moon and piling the donkey are played with the help of caps. Fly Dutchman, back scalings and grulley are played with tops. Hot rice, swolo and French foot are ball games for boys. Raps on the bugle, Polish banker and my birdie whistles are played with buttons. Eggs and bacon, stiff bloaters and sending a letter to Canada are forms of leapfrog. Daggles, hark the robbers coming through, and broken bottles are ball games for girls. French packet, London Bridge, and full stop and comma are played with marbles or stones. (I should, perhaps, have put all those games in the past tense, for Norman Douglas published his book in 1916, six years before the British Broadcasting Company came into existence, and ten before Baird gave his first practical demonstration of television. I doubt whether many of these games will have survived those two fantastic destroyers of boredom—and, perhaps, of initiative?)

Among the toys that seem almost to have disappeared are hoops and tops. Children must have been bowling hoops almost from the time of the invention of the wheel, and hoops were used by the Greeks in the gymnasium towards the end of the sixth century B.C. In Roman times they were made of metal, and were hit with a metal stick, thus adding to the many noises of the streets of Rome. The poet Martial, in the first century A.D., who would have written many angry letters to *The Times* had that newspaper existed in his day, was infuriated by these hoops, bumping noisily along the streets, and getting in the way of ordinary pedestrians. Many of them were fitted out with bells, less to warn these pedestrians than to add to the din. Greek children also played with tops, which seem to have reached England in the fourteenth century. One theory is that the top is descended from the use by primitive men of a spindle, twirled round very rapidly by a thong, in order to make a fire. I find this nearly as improbable as the theory, put forward quite seriously in one book I read, that musical chairs was invented in order to ridicule the scramble for places when there was a change of government in Britain. The use of the top is world-wide, and it seems to have been known in Peru, for example, long before Columbus discovered America.

One of the more popular of the 'war' games in the streets of London and elsewhere is, or used to be, prisoner's base. Strutt* claims that this game was first mentioned early in the reign of Edward III, in the fourteenth century, when it was banned in the neigh-bourhood of the Houses of Parliament because it in-terfered with members on their way to the House. This is another of the children's games that was subse-quently—but only temporarily—adopted by adults, for the same author describes a match in 1770 or there-abouts between twelve gentlemen of Cheshire and twelve of Derbyshire; this match took place in the fields where the Senate Building of the University of London (the Ministry of Information during the second world war) now stands.

I have already commented on the number of games that are similar in different countries. Even so English a game as oranges and lemons, with its reference to the old London churches, has its parallel in Belgium, for

* Op. cit.

example, where it is called *pommes d'or*, *pommes d'argent*. Spillikins, under the name of *les jonchets*, has been played in France since the fourteenth century. I mention tiddleywinks not because it is old–I don't know if it is–but because I like its French name, *la puce*, the flea. Claude Aveline* says that diabolo is of Chinese origin, and was sent back to France in 1772 by some missionaries in Peking. Yoyo, also imported from China, was very popular in France at the end of the eighteenth century.

According to another French book, *Les Jeux des Grecs et des Romains*,† 'apart from bicycles or tricycles, there is not a single one of our toys which had no counterpart among the Greeks or the Romans'. (This book, by the way, was published in 1891; the war toys of today would have raised some Greek and Roman eyebrows in disapproval.) Roman children had Æsop's fables; toy carriages and chariots; dolls of painted terracotta; some dolls of wax that were jointed. They had terracotta soldiers and Trojan horses in which to shut them up. They tossed coins and called 'heads' or 'ships', as there was the head of a god on one side and the reproduction of a ship on the other. There were balls of varying sizes–a *pila* was stuffed with horsehair and covered with leather or cloth; *follis* was a large, hollow ball which one struck with one's fist or forearm; *paganica* was between the two in size, but much heavier than either, and was stuffed with feathers. Balls of different sizes were much used for exercise in Roman baths, as 'medicine balls' are used today, and Caesar was one famous man who kept himself fit in this way.

As one might expect, games with marbles are of great antiquity. There are early Egyptian ones in the British Museum, and some of the small stone spheres found

* *Le Code des Jeux* (Hachette, Paris, 1961)
† Wilhelm Richter (Paris, 1891)

7(a) Cricket at Lords. Gentlemen v. players in 1841 (p. 52)

CRICKET.

A GRAND MATCH

WILL BE PLAYED IN

LORD'S GROUND,

MARYLEBONE,

On *MONDAY, JULY* 31, 1848, *& following Day.*

The Gentlemen against the Players.

PLAYERS.

Gentlemen.	Players.
Sir F. BATHURST	BOX
E. ELMHURST, Esq.	CLARK
N. FELIX, Esq.	DEAN
H. FELLOWES, Esq.	GUY
R. T. KING, Esq.	HILLYER
J. M. LEE, Esq.	LILLYWHITE
A. MYNN, Esq.	MARTINGALE
W. NICHOLSON, Esq.	PILCH
O. C. PELL, Esq.	W. PILCH
C. RIDDING, Esq.	PARR
G. YONGE, Esq.	WISDEN

MATCHES TO COME.

Wednesday, August 2nd, at Lord's—Harrow against Winchester

Thursday, August 3rd, at Lord's—Eton against Harrow

Friday, August 4th, at Lord's—Winchester against Eton

DARK'S newly-invented LEG GUARDS, also his TUBULAR and other INDIA-RUBBER GLOVES, SPIKED SOLES for CRICKET SHOES, & CRICKET BALLS, to be had of E. Dark, at the Tennis Court.

Cricket Bats and Stumps to be had of M. Dark, at the Manufactory on the Ground.

Admittance 6d.........Stabbing on the Ground.........Ordinary at 3 o'clock.

Morgan, Printer, 36, Church Street, adjoining the Marylebone Theatre.

7(b) 'Gentlemen' and 'Players' (p. 54)

8(a) Persian
hobby-horses (p. 65)

8(b) Persian polo
(p. 129)

8(c) The Romans also walked on stilts (p. 66)

among neolithic remains are thought to have been used rather for games than as projectiles. The Roman emperor Augustus used to play with his African slaves, using nuts instead of marbles (as did other Romans of his day). When I was a boy I should have felt incomplete without a few marbles in my pocket—none of them was, in fact, made of marble; the most valuable were of alabaster, the most numerous were of glass (with fascinating coloured twirls in them), the cheapest were of baked clay and, according to the *Encyclopaedia Britannica*, were sold at prices ranging from forty to a hundred a penny at the beginning of the present century. (I am told that marbles are again 'in', but not, I suspect, at that price.) From the same encyclopaedia I learn that one particular marble game 'is played by Zulu adults with great enthusiasm, and is still popular among the car-drivers of Belfast'—an unexpected example of the internationalism of pastimes! Boys at Westminster School were forbidden to play marbles in Westminster Hall because they got in the way of Members of Parliament, and undergraduates were not allowed to play on the steps of the Bodleian Library.

Another ancient toy was the hobby-horse, with a wooden horse's head fixed to a stick which one kept between one's legs. As a small boy, I thought that it was a rather silly and uncomfortable example of make-believe, but it was popular for centuries, and one sees it in many paintings of many nations from the Renaissance onwards. At its best, its framework was covered with material to cover the rider's legs and to give him the illusion that he was a gallant knight taking part in a tournament. It played a very important part in morris dances, but, as a toy, it gave way to the rocking horse in the eighteenth century, as the rocking horse gave way to the tricycle in the twentieth.

A word or two about morris dancing, which is said to

date back to John of Gaunt, who in 1336 brought over some Moorish dancers from Spain. Moorish, or the Spanish *morisco*, easily becomes morrice or morris in English. The bells worn by the dancers were originally supposed to keep the devil at a safe distance. Robin Hood, Maid Marian, Friar Tuck and others were added later to keep pace with popular legend. Morris dancers became associated with the May Day festival, and were therefore banned while the Puritans were in power. The revival of interest in folk lore and music has, of course, encouraged a revival of interest in morris dancing, but the little I have seen of it does not lead me to anticipate a revival of the rustic orgies which were formerly characteristic of the May-pole and all that.

One more pastime which kept children amused for centuries but which has now almost disappeared is that of walking on stilts. Stilts have been used by children or adults in many parts of the world and over many centuries. Maya Indians of Yucatan danced on stilts to please the bird deity, Yaccocahmut. To come nearer home, but farther away in time, stilts were well-known in ancient Rome, and some writers have suggested that the habit of walking on stilts gave rise to the legend of the Titans, whose ill-treatment by their father, Saturn, was avenged by their mother in a manner not to be described in a book which is unfashionably designed to shock nobody.

Kite-flying is very old (and not only in the political sense). The first known kite-maker in Europe was Archytas, an astronomer of Taranto, in southern Italy. He is supposed also to have invented the screw, the pulley and a wooden pigeon that could fly. He lived in the fifth century B.C., but it is now generally agreed that kites were being flown many centuries earlier in East Asia, where they are still very popular and where they are flown almost as often by adults as by children. Originally, their flight probably had a religious significance, as it still has among the Maoris of New Zealand. On the ninth day of the ninth month, Chinese men and boys stream out to open spaces to fly their kites. Many of these kites carry perforated lengths of bamboo, and the wind passing through them makes weird and dismal noises which are supposed to frighten away evil spirits. So are the men, often dolled up as prostitutes, who walk on stilts behind a Chinese coffin to distract these spirits from the corpse.

Korea, Japan and the countries of South-east Asia share this Chinese love of kite-flying. Up the east coast of Malaya, where there are very few Chinese, the Malays for generations have held kite-flying competitions. A competitor tries to get to windward of his opponent and to cut his cord with a sharp jerk of his own cord, which has been roughened and toughened by glue and splinters of porcelain or glass.

*   *   *

The ancient Greeks, as we are reminded by the Olympic Games, paid the greatest possible attention to physical fitness, and they did so as much for religious as for national reasons. Sickly or deformed children had small prospects of survival–the father of every child had absolute freedom to decide whether an infant should be 'exposed', left out in the cold to die. If his decision was favourable, there was a congratulatory party five days after the infant's birth, and a crown of olive twigs (in the case of a boy) or a ribbon (in the case of a girl) was hung over the door. A few days later there was another celebration, when the child was given its name.

The most famous illustration of Greek interest in physical fitness was, of course, the success of the Olympic Games. They are said either to have celebrated Jupiter's victory over the Titans, and to date back to 1453 B.C., or to have been instituted by Hercules in 1222 B.C. Orisippos, in the 15th Olympiad, was the first competitor to run naked—he lost his shorts in the middle of a race—and subsequently even the presidents and the judges were generally in that state. Except for the priestess of Demeter, women were excluded, and gate-crashers were thrown off a high rock. Only Greeks and Romans were allowed to compete—'barbarians' were allowed only to watch—and competitors had to train for at least ten months in the gymnasium of Elis, in the Peloponnesus. However great their athletic skill, they were barred unless they were men of good character, and were able to swear, in front of a statue of Zeus, that they had committed no murder or act of sacrilege. Games on this serious and religious level were first mentioned after the death of Patroclus, a Greek leader who was killed by Hector during the siege of Troy—Achilles avenged this death by killing not only twelve young Trojan prisoners but also four of his horses and two of his dogs. He then ended the funeral ceremony with a display of 'funeral games'.

With a few gaps—one Olympiad, for example, had to be postponed for three years since Nero's workmen had not finished the huge palace in which he proposed to accommodate it—the Olympic Games were carried on for twelve centuries. The games were abolished in A.D. 393 by the Emperor Theodosius, mainly because he was a Christian and the games were too obviously pagan in their origin; orders were given for the destruction of all pagan temples in the Eastern Empire, and this order included the temple of Olympia. The plain where the games had been held became thickly covered with sand, washed down from the surrounding mountains. When at last the sand was cleared away again, the excavators found more than a hundred statues and large quantities of bronzes, terracotta figures and thousands of coins.

In the earliest Olympics, the only event was a race over a distance of some two hundred yards–one lap of the stadium. Longer races and other events were added after the thirteenth Games. For the long jump, competitors were allowed to give themselves extra momentum by swinging heavy dumb-bells which they dropped as they took off. Wrestlers were smothered with oil and then sprinkled with sand. Boxers had their fists bound round with strips of leather–typically, in the Roman games lead or iron studs were included.

After the sixth Olympiad, the only prize was an olive garland from a specially sacred tree, but amateur status seems to have been as difficult to regulate as it is today. An Athenian victor, for example, received 500 drachmae and free meals for the rest of his life. The reward for a Spartan was less attractive–the place of honour in a battle. Victors often had altars built in their honour, and in at least one case a special breach was made in the city wall so that the hero might not be compelled to pass through the ordinary gate like an ordinary man.

When Rome replaced Athens as the centre of the civilised world, the Games continued, but on a very different footing. They were preceded by processions much less religious than the Greek ones had been and the competitors had become professionals. In Greece, the highest in the land had been proud to compete; in Rome, the nation's leaders were more likely to loll in their boxes while professional charioteers or gladiators competed in the arena below. Originally, the gladiators had been part of the ceremonies in honour of the dead, and the first reference to them was in 264 B.C., when they were brought in by the sons of Decimus Junius Brutus to honour the memory of their father. But after the stern republic had given way to the effete empire, gladiatorial combats—with free issues of wheat or bread—became part of the 'bread and circuses' designed to make the masses indifferent to the fact that they had no say whatsoever in the government of their country. Sometimes an emperor would take some part in the games, and on one occasion Nero, dressed in green livery, had the soil of the arena covered with green copper oxide instead of sand. But such escapades brought no credit to the empire, the emperor or the games.

The Circus Maximus, where most games and races were held, is said to have seated 350,000 spectators, and members of the public backed their particular team of charioteers, in white, red, blue or green tunics, with as much enthusiasm as do spectators on Epsom Downs—the major difference being that entertainment was laid on for the Romans on at least half the days of the year.

*   *   *

To revert to more modern and less bloody occupations, the Olympic Games, as we now know them, are due to the initiative of a Frenchman, Baron Pierre de Coubertin, who, with the co-operation of representatives of the English Amateur Athletic Association and the American Athletic Union, organised an international conference in Paris in 1894. The conference, attended by men from France, Great Britain, the United States, Sweden, Italy, Spain, Greece, Russia and Belgium, decided that Games should be held every four years, as they had been in ancient Greece, and the first modern Olympiad was held in Athens in 1896. More than seventy nations are now represented on the International Olympic Committee. The reader must decide for himself to what extent the harassed members of this Committee are successful in diminishing the suicidal tendencies of nationalism in an atomic world.

CHAPTER SIX

Golf, Gouffe, Gowff or Goff

Golf, Scottish or Dutch? · Paganica *and* cambuca · *Scots and Sunday golf* · *The demands of archery* · *Rabbits on the tees* · *Smollett on golf* · *The nineteenth hole*

GOLF, gouffe, gowff or goff—for 'goff' is not, as I had imagined, a mere modern affectation—is claimed by Robert Clark* to be 'a game peculiar to the Scots'. As recently as 1922, when the leaders of Europe were trying to settle their affairs at San Remo, Mr Lloyd George very nearly lost M. Aristide Briand his job as French premier by persuading him to try his arm at golf—the French found if difficult to accept the idea that they should be governed by a man who was photographed while hitting, or trying to hit, a small ball on a course made for the amusement of irresponsible people like the Anglo-Saxons. Neither of the participants in that memorable game was Scottish, and any claim today that golf was 'peculiar to the Scots' would be as absurd as one that football was peculiar to the English. To give one example, the prime ministers of Malaysia and of Singapore, the one a Malayan prince and the other a Chinese Socialist, have come nearer to agreement on the golf course at Kuala Lumpur or the Cameron Highlands than in any office. But was the game ever 'peculiar to the Scots?'

According to the *Encyclopaedia Britannica*, 'it is scarcely to be doubted that the game is of Dutch origin'. The *Book of Hours*, published in Bruges early in the sixteenth century but now in the British Museum, has an illustration of a foursome, with the players putting

---

* *Golf: A Royal and Ancient Game* (Macmillan, London, 1893)

71

at a hole in the turf in a game called '*Het Kolving*', or 'The golf'. In several other engravings or woodcuts from the Low Countries, they are putting on ice at a stick—admittedly a strange form of golf. The French *Encyclopédie Larousse* suggests that the game was introduced into England, in the form of *pallemail*, by 'the companions of William the Conqueror'. My own edition of Larousse, an early one but unfortunately undated, has an unexpected list of the hazards a golfer must face. 'Streams, rivers, ploughed fields, quarries, copses, woods, walls, railways and even houses—all are good for the purpose.'

In an earlier chapter, I mentioned a reference in an Anglo-French dictionary of 1611 to a *crosse* as a club 'used in French Flanders at the local kind of golf', and it is a fact that for a long time the Scots were compelled to buy their golf balls in Holland. (The very name, golf, is generally believed to come from the German *Kolbe*, a club, which became *Kolf* in Low Dutch.) In 1618, to put an end to this humiliating dependence on the Netherlands, King James I of England (James VI of Scotland) gave a firm in Edinburgh the monopoly for twenty-one years for the manufacture of golf balls since 'thair is no small quantitie of gold and siluer transported zierlie out of His Hienes kingdome of Scotland for bying of golf ballis'.

Not surprisingly, Robert Clark indignantly rejects any suggestion that golf originated in Holland. 'There is evidence', he writes, 'that early in the fifteenth century it was *popular* [in Scotland] in such a sense as it can scarcely at this day claim to be; and the obvious inference from this is that its *origin* lies very much further back—perhaps in the prehistoric period.'

Another Scottish writer, Sir Guy Campbell,* has suggested that golf was probably introduced into Great

* *A History of Golf in Great Britain* (Cassell, London, 1952)

Britain by Roman soldiers, in much the same way as British soldiers took with them rugby football and cricket to remote parts of the world. One weakness of this theory, however, seems to be that the Romans never conquered Scotland, and all the evidence shows that golf was first played north of the border and of Hadrian's wall.

Undoubtedly, the Dutch game differed very widely from our present golf. It was played on a ground roughly the size of a tennis court, and the ball was a heavy one, about the size of a cricket ball. It might, more accurately, be compared with the 'mini-golf' one finds at every seaside resort. (In 1456 a decree forbad Dutch citizens to play it in churches or churchyards.) But Campbell does not try to minimise the similarities between the Dutch and the Scottish games. He mentions a well-known painting by the Dutch artist, Aelbert Cuyp, dated 1650, in which a girl in an attractive, but most unsuitable, blue satin dress is about to use an iron not unlike the wooden-shafted irons used in Britain before the first world war. He also refers to another picture, painted sixteen years later by Adriaen Van de Velde, of two Dutchmen playing in a foursome with two men in kilts. An early international match between Scotland and the Netherlands?

There was another variety of the game which was played in Flanders from the fourteenth century onwards. In this, an attacker had to hit a post or some other chosen mark in the lowest possible number of strokes. He was allowed three strokes to one by the defender. But, by this one stroke, the defender drove the ball into the most difficult positions. A game, in fact, probably closer to croquet than to golf.

Strutt* claims that golf 'answers to a rustic pastime of the Romans, which they played with a ball of leather

* Op. cit.

stuffed with feathers, called *paganica*, and the goff-ball is composed of the same material to this day'. In the reign of Edward III, golf was sometimes known by the Latin name, *cambuca*, owing to the crooked club with which it was played. In fact, golf did not have very much in common with either *paganica* or *cambuca*, but doubtless many Scots would prefer to believe their national game came from the ancient Romans than from the relatively modern Dutch or Flemings. And yet the Dutch game was a test of accuracy, in that the ball had to hit a mark (or, in golf, to fall into a hole) and the Flemish game was a test of long-distance (or, in golf, getting on to the green in the lowest number of strokes). Even though the early Scottish golfers had the humiliation of buying their golf balls from Holland, they can with justification boast that they took the best features of both games of the Low Countries.

*　　*　　*

The first definite mention of golf in the British Isles seems to have been in 1457, when the Scottish parliament decreed that 'fute-ball and golf be utterly cryit doune and noch usit'. Instead, it was decreed that 'schutting [shooting] be usit ilk Sunday'. Whereas similar decisions were being enforced in England lest English archers should be out-matched by the French, the Scottish decrees were enforced 'to strengthen Scotland against oure auld ennimies of England'. It was also considered necessary that every yeoman who could not be trained effectively to use a bow should have 'a gude ax and a targe of leddir to resist the shot of Ingland'. In 1491, James IV confirmed the decree that 'in no place of the realme there be usit fute-ball, golfe, or uther sik unprofitabill sportis'. The decree was not very effective; in a letter dated August 13th, 1513, to Cardinal Wolsey, Catherine of Aragon wrote that all the King's subjects were 'busy with the golfe'.

By degrees the motive behind these bans was changed. It had less to do with the safety of the state than with the souls of its citizens. In 1592, the Edinburgh town council forbad 'ony pastymes or gammis within or without the toun upon the Sabbath day sik as golf, aircherie, row-bowllis, penny stane, kactch pullis or sic other'. The order also laid down that 'their dochteris and women servends be nocht fund playing at the ball nor singing profayne sangs upoun the sam day'. Later, this pro-hibition was limited to 'the tyme of sermons', and the records of many Scottish towns mention fines or terms of imprisonment imposed upon people for playing games 'in the time of preaching'.

It was James VI of Scotland who took pity on the people. In 1618, he ordered that 'our good people be not disturbed letted or discouraged from any lawfull recreation—such as dauncing, either for men or women, archerie for men, leaping . . . or other such harmless recreation' after the end of Sunday service, since their work during the week gave them so little time for amusements.

The Stuart kings, in common with the kings of England and France, did not impose restrictions on themselves by these orders. Charles I played golf while he was a prisoner (of the Scots) at Newcastle, and he was playing golf at Leith when the news arrived of the outbreak of the Irish rebellion—the evidence is con-flicting as to whether, like Drake on Plymouth Hoe, he postponed action until he had ended his game. In the previous century, both James IV and James V of Scotland had been golfers, and it was rumoured (but possibly only by her enemies) that Mary Stuart was seen playing golf and pall-mall a few days after the murder of her husband, Lord Darnley.

The early golf courses were naturally very different from those of today. The first links in Great Britain were at Leith, and had only five holes, but the distances between the holes varied from 414 to 495 yards. There were no well-cultivated greens, the shortness of the turf depending mainly upon the number and the appetites of the local rabbits—in 1552, a licence was granted to John Hamilton ('Johne be the mercie of God Archbishop of Sanctandros') to put his rabbits on the links of St Andrews 'and to use thame to our itilitie and pleasour'.

Sir Guy Campbell writes that in 1681 or 1682, James II, when Duke of York, accepted a challenge from two English noblemen to a match in Edinburgh to decide whether golf was a Scottish or an English game. The Duke could choose any Scottish partner he liked, and he chose a shoemaker called John Paterson—a reminder of the fact that, at least in Scotland, golf was always a democratic game. James and John won hands down. It is also interesting that the decree whereby James I gave the monopoly for the manufacture of golf balls to a man in Edinburgh was issued from Salisbury. It is therefore probable that, at least under the Stuarts, the game was known in England. This knowledge, however, seems almost to have disappeared with them, and the game became 'Royal' only in the early years of the nineteenth century at the behest of William IV, an English king of German origin.

Even so, it must have been very little known south of the Tweed, for Smollett wrote that 'the citizens of Edinburgh divert themselves at a game called golf, in which they use a curious kind of bats tipped with horn, and small elastic balls stuffed with feathers. . . . These they strike with such force and dexterity from one hole to another that they will fly to an incredible distance.' He added that the players 'never went to bed without having each the best part of a gallon of claret in his belly'.

This last statement is libellous—at least, the drink now would be whisky or beer—but the 'nineteenth hole' nevertheless seems to be an old-established institution. In the minutes of the Musselburgh Golf Club for January 11th, 1793, there is one to this effect: 'The meeting was so merry that it was agreed that matching and every other business should be delayed until next month.'

CHAPTER SEVEN

'Game and Playe of the Chesse'

Chess and Caxton · Evilmerodach, King of Babylon · Who invented chess? · The tutor and the grains of barley · Chess 'gamesmanship' · Draughts

THE two best-known games in the world, I suppose, are chess for the intellectuals and football for the athletes. Of the former game, so much has been written by so many experts that references to it by anybody whose knowledge is confined to two or three opening gambits may seem impertinent. But so many other games are in some way connected with chess that one cannot omit it from a book on pastimes. *Hamlet* without the Prince of Denmark.

It is the only game in the world, somebody has pointed out, in which luck plays no part at all. (It does play some part, however, since the man who has first move has an advantage.) Praises of it are innumerable and almost universal. Falkener* wrote that 'as mathematics is a handmaid of logic, and teaches the lawyer to build up and establish his proofs before he goes on, so chess teaches the soldier not merely the science of attack, but instils caution in the mind of the prudent general to avoid surprise, to fortify his base of operations and to despise no foe'. The second book to be printed in the English language was *Game and Playe of the Chesse*, which was printed in 1474, while Caxton was still living in Bruges. (A copy of this was once bought for the equivalent of twopence from a bookstall in Holland by a collector who, according to Sir Walter

---

* *Games Ancient and Oriental and How to Play Them* (Longmans Green, London, 1892)

Scott, was 'commonly called Snuffy Wilson, from his inveterate addiction to black rapee'. How, with such an example in mind, can one pass any bookstall? Only eleven copies of this book are known to exist but one of them might be there, between some much-thumbed detective story and some unread volume of sermons.)

Caxton translated his treatise on chess from a French book which, in turn, had been translated from the Latin. The author was an Italian, a Dominican monk known as Jacobus de Cessolis, who lived towards the end of the twelfth century. He had used the game as the inspiration for many sermons, emphasising the duty of each piece on the board towards the other pieces, and ending with the fate of the king who is checkmated when he loses the support of his subjects. In the book, the invention of chess is attributed to a Greek philosopher, Philometer, who was adviser to Evilmerodach, son of Nebuchadnezzar and king of Babylon in the sixth century B.C. Evilmerodach is described as 'a jolye man with oute Justice and so cruell that he dyde hewe his faders body in thre honderd pieces, and gaf it to ete and devour to thre honderd birdes that men call vultres'. Caxton's second edition, printed in 1450, has a splendid woodcut, in which the vultures—looking singularly like doves—are carrying away practically all of the unfortunate father, leaving only one leg and his head, still surmounted by a crown.

According to the Dominican author, Evilmerodach saw some of his knights playing chess, and ordered Philometer to teach him the game. In the process of learning it, he had to listen to detailed lectures on the duty of each piece. The knight, for example, 'ought to be made alle armed upon an hors in such wyse that he haue an helm on his heed and a spere in his ryght hande'. The rook's pawn should be 'a man of the comyn peple on fote . . . holding in his right hande a spade or

79

a shouell and a rodde in his lefte hande'. The knight's pawn should represent a blacksmith, since a knight needs 'bridellys sadellys speres and other thynges made by the handes of the smythes'. The king's pawn should hold in his right hand a pair of scales and a weight in his left, 'and at his gurdell a purse full of monoye for to gyve to them that requyre hit'. The queen's pawn represents 'the phisicyan, spicer and Apotyquaire' with, at his girdle, 'his instrumentys of yron and siluer for to make Incysions and to serche woundes and hurtes and to cut apostumes'.

The king's bishop's pawn represents the 'tauerners, hostelers and sellers of vitaylle'. Next to it comes the representative of city watchmen and guards, with keys, a pot and a measure. Inspired by all these and other explanations, Evilmerodach became a reformed man, 'juste and vertuous, debonayre, gracious and full of vertues unto alle peple. And a man that lyuyth in this world without vertues liueth not as a man but as a beste.' To make the lesson clearer, the board was made with sixty-four squares, to represent the squares into which Babylon was divided, and at one corner there was a tower to represent the Tower of Babel.

In the early days of chess, the place of the present queen was taken, although with much less power, by a vizier, or minister. The Persian name, 'firz', became latinised into 'farzia' or 'fercia'. In French, this became, in one version, 'fierge', and the *Encyclopaedia Britannica* suggests that 'fierge' might easily have become *vierge*, which could explain the change of sex from vizier to queen. Others, and in particular Mr Willard Fiske, of whom more later, treat this suggestion with contempt, but they do not explain the uncontrovertible fact that, however created, the queen appeared on the chess boards of Europe only towards the end of the fifteenth century.

9 Small boy golfer. The Dutch version (p. 72)

10(a) Adriaen Van de Velde's 'Golfers on the Ice near Haarlem' in the National Gallery, London (p. 72)

10(b) Golf fashions in 1891 (p. 71 et seq.)

One could, of course, fill many pages with notable quotations in favour of chess. I was rather glad to come across somebody who wrote critically of the game. I have already mentioned Baldassare Castiglione, whose book, *The Courtier*, was every young man's guide to etiquette at the court of the Dukes of Urbino in the sixteenth century. He wrote that chess was 'certainly a pleasing and ingenious amusement . . . but it seems to me to have one defect, which is that it is possible to have too much knowledge of it, so that whoever would excel in the game must give a great deal of time to it, as I believe, and as much study as if he would learn some noble science or perform well anything of importance; and yet, in the end, for all his pains, he only knows how to play a game. Thus, I think, a very unusual thing happens in this, namely that mediocrity is more to be praised than excellence.' Which is very comforting to those of us whose chess is, at best, mediocre.

Who invented chess? According to one legend, Xerxes, King of Persia. If that were so, one would have to abandon the Evilmerodach legend, for Xerxes fought the Spartans at Thermopylae in 480 B.C., whereas Evilmerodach ruled in Babylon from 562 to 560 B.C., and it is in the highest degree unlikely that so young a man could have taught so complicated a game to so old a man. But Jacobus de Cessolis claims that Xerxes was the Chaldean name for the Greek Philometer, and for all I know he may have been right.

In any case, there are many other claimants. I have already mentioned the story according to which dice were invented by Palamedes, to keep his Greek soldiers occupied during the siege of Troy. With the same end in view he is supposed to have invented chess and backgammon. Another claimant is Ulysses himself, who, by one of the shabbier tricks in mythology, had Palamedes murdered because he had revealed that

Ulysses was shamming madness in order to keep out of the Trojan war. Then there was the wife of Ravana, a king of Ceylon, who hoped that the game would keep her husband's mind occupied while his capital was being besieged by Rama 'in the second age of the world'. Nor does the list end here. Claims have been put forward on behalf of the Egyptians, the Jews, the Scythians, the Araucanians (natives of Chile), the Hindus, the Chinese, the Arabs, the Castilians, the Irish and the Welsh. According to the *Encyclopaedia Britannica*, the Irish version does not seem to have been a sedentary game at all; unfortunately, it does not go on to tell us how the game was played.

A strange little book by H. E. Bird,* who was one of the greatest chess players in Britain in the second half of the last century, makes some extraordinary claims or quotes other people who have made them. For example, those two great pioneers of medicine, Hippocrates and Galen, are said to have believed that chess was a cure for several complaints, including diarrhoea and erysipelas. And he quotes a tenth-century writer, Zakaria Yahyd, for the statement that chess was played by 'Aristotle, by Yafet ibn Nuh (Japhet, son of Noah), by Solomon for the loss of his son, and even by Adam when he grieved for Abel'. From which I conclude that one of the outstanding qualities of chess is to stimulate the imagination of its enthusiasts.

* * *

The most widely-accepted version is that chess came to us from Northern India by way of Persia. A very famous German scholar, Dr A. Van der Linde,† put forward the theory that it was invented by Buddhists in India in order to turn men's minds away from war.

* *Chess History and Reminiscences* (Dean, London, 1893)
† *Geschichte und Litteratur des Schachspiels* (Berlin, 1870)

Buddhists are also supposed to have taken the game with them to China—in which case, their primary objective does not seem to have been reached, since the Chinese name for chess meant 'The Play of the Science of War' and it was considered as a useful training in military strategy. Indeed, as such it has been almost universally treated. Most historians agree with Van der Linde that the game was invented in India, but attribute it rather to the Hindus than to the Buddhists.

Another legend about the origin of the game in India is that a Brahmin tutor invented it in order to impress upon a young prince the fact that, although the king was the most important piece on the board, it could do nothing without the co-operation of the other pieces— the same lesson, in fact, as was later taught by the Dominican monk whose book was translated and printed by William Caxton. The young prince was so pleased by this method of learning the facts of monarchical life that he offered his tutor any reward he cared to name. The tutor asked for no money; his request appeared to be a modest one—one grain of barley on the first square of the chessboard, two on the second, four on the third, eight on the fourth, and so on until the sixty-fourth square was reached. The request lost its air of modesty once the court mathematicians had worked it out. They concluded that the number of grains would be 18,446,744,073,709,551,615, and that there was not that much barley in the country. At two shillings a bushel, so I am assured, this would cost £3,385,966,239,667. I must confess that I have not myself worked out these sums, but I am confident that nobody else will do so. I also confess that, had I been the young prince, I should immediately have sacked a tutor who had made me look such a fool.

The Persian claim is a strong one, but etymologists argue that the names of some of the pieces and of the game itself make them doubt whether the game originated in Persia. There is, too, the story that envoys from India arrived one day at the court of the Persian king, Chosroes I, in the sixth century, with a chess board and a message to the effect that the Persian must either master the game or pay tribute to their own king. In any event, it seems to have been from the Persians that the Arabs learned their chess, and it was probably the Arabs who brought the game to Spain. Alternative theories are, one, that chess was brought back to Europe by the crusaders, with the rest of their loot from the Holy Land, and, two, that it came to Italy by way of Byzantium. 'Checkmate' is said to be derived from two Arabic words, '*Schach mat*', meaning 'the king is dead'.

Murray's* time-table is as follows. The game was invented in India about A.D. 570. It reached Persia before 600, and was taken over by the Moslem conquerors of Persia by 650. They had spread a knowledge of the game in Egypt by 720 and, via Morocco, in Spain by 750. Christians were playing chess in Spain by 1010, in Italy and southern Germany by 1050, in France before 1070, and in England before 1100. The Byzantine Empire knew chess by 800, and the game spread from Constantinople to Russia. Some years earlier, the Mongols had learnt it from the Hindus, and in all probability the Chinese had learnt it from the Mongols. From China, it passed on to Japan and, in the eleventh century, to Siam and other countries of South-east Asia. Despite the various claims that it was invented by the Greeks, it does not seem to have been played in ancient Greece, and the only reference I have come across to a knowledge of chess in ancient Rome is to the effect that Aenobarbus and Coecilius Metullus Dalmatus, consuls

* *A History of Board Games other than Chess* by H. J. R. Murray (Clarendon Press, Oxford, 1952)

in 115 B.C., prohibited almost all public entertainments except those of flute players and all games of chance except chess and draughts. But most experts agree that chess was invented in India nearly seven hundred years after this date, and that draughts dates from the eleventh or twelfth century; the two Roman consuls were obviously favouring some other board games altogether.

If we accept Murray's time-table, we must abandon several attractive theories, some of which I have already mentioned. It rules out such alleged originators as Solomon, Japheth, Shem, Xerxes, Aristotle and Semiramis. It would even contradict the story in St Olave's saga to the effect that King Canute, who died in 1035, was a keen player, and that Earl Ulf, who angrily upset the chess board during a game with Canute in Denmark, was murdered next morning in Roskilde church by the king's order. Almost certainly they, too, were playing some other board game.

The Hindus called chess *chaturanga*, which the Arabs turned into *shatranj*. In its earliest days, there were four players, each with eight pieces of which four were pawns, and the element of chance was not entirely excluded, since dice were thrown to decide which piece must be moved. Presumably, the game acquired its fascination for intellectuals only after the use of dice had been forbidden—as it was at one time or another in most countries, in the hope of lessening mankind's passion for gambling; the eradication of this element of chance led to the invention of the many opening gambits which so alarm the beginner.

This is not the place in which to follow in detail the evolution of chess, about which so many books have been written, but something must be said about three of the pieces—the king, the rook and the bishop. The king used to be the most mobile piece on the board—he could move three squares at a time – and his power lessened as that of the vizier (later, the queen) increased, almost as though the game were preparing the way for the change from kings by divine right to constitutional monarchs. The piece the Anglo-Saxons (and the Icelanders) call the 'bishop' has experienced remarkable changes, apart from its increased mobility from two squares to the diagonal length of the board. The Persians called this piece '*pil*', or the 'elephant'. The Arabs, having no 'p' in their alphabet, called it '*fil*', which, preceded by the definite article, became '*al-fil*'. The Italians turned this into '*alfiere*', a 'standard-bearer', and call it by that name to the present time. In France, it became the '*fol*', and then the '*fou*' – the fool or the joker. In England, after a period as the 'archer', it became the 'bishop'. More understandably, in view of the distances it can cover, it became in Germany the '*Laufer*', or 'runner'.

But apparently, before the Indian game had been taken over by the Persians, the name 'elephant' was used in connection with the rook, and not with the bishop. 'The rare and very modern usage which occasionally makes the rook an "elephant" ', writes Fiske,* 'is derived from its name in the oft-reprinted and oft-translated Latin poem (1525) of Girolamo Vida . . . who calls it *elephantus turritus*, or "towered elephant".' This ultimately led to the adoption of the title of 'tower' for the rook in several languages, or castle in English. Among the several twelfth-century rooks in the Bargello Museum in Florence, there is one in the shape of an elephant. I refer to the conjunction of elephant and castle in a later chapter.

To keep pace with the changes in the names of the pieces on the chess board, there have, of course, also

* *Chess in Iceland* by Willard Fiske (Florence, 1905)

been considerable changes in the rules. Little seems to be known about the four-handed chess already mentioned. The Chinese variety of the game is said to have been invented some two centuries before Christ, and there is even a claim, recorded in the annals of the Royal Asiatic Society, that it was played in China, with 360 pieces, as far back in history as 2300 B.C. Few people, however, would take this claim very seriously–the Chinese undoubtedly made great contributions to the development of civilisation, but not quite as many as they are accustomed to claim. In Chinese chess, the king and two counsellors remained in a fortress consisting of four squares. Their chariots–the rooks of today–were stationed at the four corners of the board. The elephants, as with the bishops of today, were near the king and his counsellors. Between them and the chariots were the horses, in front of which were the guns. A river, one square wide, ran across the middle of the board to divide the two armies; it could be crossed by the horses, but not by the elephants. The infantry, as with our pawns, could advance one square at a time, and the river counted as one square. Thus it will be seen that Chinese chess had many points in common with the chess we play today. Japanese chess, on the other hand, was very different. It was played on a board of nine by ten squares, and it was unusual in that captured pieces were at once put to fight on the side of their captor. The knight, in our chess, was replaced by the horse. They had chariots instead of castles, thus giving some colour to the theory that chariots were the original rooks.

* * *

It would be strange if a game which achieved such popularity had not attracted the attention of Haroun al-Raschid, caliph of Baghdad towards the end of the

eighth century. One story about him is to the effect that
the Byzantine emperor Nicephorus I wrote him a letter
in which he said: 'The Empress [Irene] into whose
place I have succeeded, looked upon yourself as a *Rukh*,
and herself as a mere pawn. Therefore she submitted to
pay you a tribute more than the double of which she
ought to have exacted from you. All this has been owing
to female weakness and timidity. Now, however, I in-
sist that you, immediately on reading this letter, repay
me all the sums you ever received from her. If you
hesitate, the sword shall settle our accounts.'

To this somewhat discourteous letter, Haroun – according to Arab sources – sent a reply that was both curt
and masterly. 'In the name of God, the merciful and
gracious', it ran. 'From Haroun, the commander of the
faithful, to the Roman dog, Nicephorus. I have read
thine epistle, thou son of an infidel mother; my answer
to it thou shalt see, not hear.' He immediately marched
his armies westwards and compelled Nicephorus to beg
for peace. In a less belligerent mood, Haroun is alleged
to have sent a very fine set of ivory chessmen to
Charlemagne, who was a keen chess player, but who
does not seem to have developed all the finer qualities
that chess is said to inculcate; there is a French phrase
for somebody who leaves the gaming table as soon as
he has made substantial winnings – '*faire Charlemagne*'.

Although chess is much less likely than most other
games to encourage betting, the attitude of the clergy
to it was at first hostile. A few years before the Norman
conquest of England, St Peter Damian wrote to Pope
Alexander II to say that he had punished a Florentine
bishop for playing chess in public. It was inconsistent
with his duty, he told the bishop, 'to sport away thy
evenings amidst the vanity of chess, and defile the hand
which offers up the body of the Lord, and the tongue
that mediates between God and man, with the pollution

of a sacriligious game'. The bishop was ordered to wash the feet of twelve poor persons and to give them liberal alms. At one time, 'clerks playing at dice or chess' were, *ipso facto*, excommunicated. Rather more understandably, John Huss deeply reproached himself for having wasted time and risked violent passions by playing the game.

Other players had fewer prickings of conscience. After Canute, William the Conqueror, Henry I, John, Edward I and Charles I were among the kings of England who are said to have been keen players. Charles, indeed, is reported to have been involved in a game of chess when the letter arrived to inform him that the Scots had agreed to hand him over to the Parliamentary forces. (I have already mentioned that he was playing golf at Leith when he heard the news of the outbreak of the Irish rebellion. How he reacted on that occasion is not known, but he went on with his game of chess 'with the same placidity of manner and apparent interest, as if the letter had remained unopened'.*) King John showed a similar *sang froid* when messengers arrived from Rouen to announce the grave news that their city was being besieged by King Philip of France—they had to wait until His Majesty had finished his game.

Being so much a game of kings, it is perhaps natural that it should be surrounded by a certain amount of etiquette. But one book† I have come across would seem to me to contain a good deal of superfluous advice about behaviour towards one's opponent. 'You should not sing, nor whistle, not look at your watch, not take up a book to read, nor make a tapping with your feet on the floor nor with your fingers on the table, nor do anything

* *Memoirs of the Court of England during the Reign of the Stuarts* by J. Heneage Jesse (Bentley, London, 1840)

† *Chess Potpourri* by Alfred C. Klahre (Brooklyn, New York, 1931)

that may disturb his attention. . . . You ought not to endeavour to amuse and deceive your adversary by pretending to have made bad moves, and saying that you have now lost the game in order to make him secure and careless and inattentive to your schemes; for this is fraud and deceit, not skill in the game.' It may be fraud and deceit, but it is also Gamesmanship worthy of my friend, Stephen Potter.

Having defeated your opponent, Klahre goes on, 'you must not use any triumphing or insulting expression, nor show too much pleasure. You should console him by some such expression as "you understand the game better than I, but you are a little inattentive".' I have some doubts whether such an expression would be conducive to good relations, but his counsel to a spectator seems to be more sensible. 'If you give advice, you offend both parties—him against whom you give it, because it may cause the loss of his game, him in whose favour you give it, because, though it be good and he follows it, he loses the pleasure he might have had if you had permitted him to think until it had occurred to himself. Even after a move or moves, you must not, by replacing the pieces, show how it might have been played better; for that displeases both, and may occasion disputes and doubts about their true situation.' No wonder the Chinese called chess 'the play of the science of war'!

*　　*　　*

A chapter on chess must obviously end with a few paragraphs about draughts, which some writers believe to be the older of the two games. Not so the dogmatic and extremely discursive Mr Willard Fiske (the 'stray notes' that accompany his *Chess in Iceland** cover 330 pages of very small type, and death overtook him before

* Op. cit.

he could get down to a second volume). 'Whatever else is known with certainty as to the story of chess', he writes, 'this is at any rate sure, that the game existed long before draughts came into being.' The *Encyclopaedia Britannica*, on the other hand, writes that a somewhat similar game to draughts—in America, checkers—was being played in Egypt some thirty-five centuries ago; 'men', or pieces, have been found in tombs dating from 1600 B.C., and part of Queen Hatshepsut's draughts board (but not, alas, any loaded dice) can be seen in the British Museum. There is also an Egyptian vase there on which one can see a lion and an antelope playing a form of draughts, each with five men. This Egyptian game presumably developed later into the Roman *ludus latrunculorum*, or 'game of robbers', about which I shall be writing in a later chapter. But this must have differed very widely from the draughts that became immensely popular in Europe during and after the Renaissance. The popularity of the game in Scotland seems to have been one of the consequences of the Thirty Years War; so many Scots learned to play it while they were serving in the Protestant forces in the Netherlands.

There is today a confusing variety of draughts, with the British playing what is known as 'French draughts' and the French playing what is known as 'Polish draughts', which the Poles themselves subsequently adopted as the French game—apparently the Polish game was invented in Paris in 1727 or thereabouts, and according to some sources the inventor's name was Polonais. To make matters more complicated, what the French call 'English draughts' is the game that was played by the French themselves, on a board with sixty-four squares, until the eighteenth century. There are many other varieties—Spanish, Canadian, Indian, Swedish, Russian, Turkish and so on—some of which can be placed in one of two categories; they are either *le jeu plaisant*, in which one was not compelled to take an enemy 'man' if one did not want to, and *le jeu forcé*, or *forçat*, in which one was 'huffed' if one failed to do so. 'Huffing' – '*soufflage*' in French – was made compulsory in the sixteenth century, and greatly raised the intellectual standard of the game.

A game with several similarities to draughts was very popular in ancient Greece, and Homer, in the Odyssey, describes how Penelope's suitors played it while they were trying to persuade her that Ulysses was dead and that she had best select one of them as his successor. In one Greek version of the game, each player had five men on a board of twenty-five squares; in another, there were four men a side, sixteen squares, and a 'sacred enclosure' in the middle of the board. In the Roman *ludus latrunculorum*, one man could jump over another, as in modern draughts, the object being not to remove an enemy from the board, but to imprison him by one's own men on every side. In Egypt and in Greece, the men were called 'dogs', as was also the case in their chess, and the lowest score with dice.

The name, 'draughts' is said to come from the Anglo-Saxon *dragan*, to draw (although I still don't know why). It is called *le jeu des dames* in France, *el juego de damas* in Spain and *Damenspiel* in German, and one theory is that it was given this name because it was contemptuously considered as a kind of chess for women. But it seems quite probable that the name has nothing to do with women at all; it may come from the German '*Damm*', or rampart. Chaucer wrote of 'draughtes' as 'a move at the chesse', and Caxton referred to 'the progressyon and draughtes of the forsayd playe of the chesse'. The name might therefore mean no more than 'a game which is a series of moves'.

The tendency to treat the game as one for children also has no historical justification. Samuel Johnson once wrote that the game 'is peculiarly calculated to fix the attention without straining it', but there are seven possible first moves and to each of them there are seven possible replies. Torquemada, the Spanish Dominican friar who established the Spanish inquisition in the fifteenth century – not a man to waste time in trifling occupations – took draughts so seriously that he wrote a book about it, and the French philosopher Diderot, in the eighteenth century, is said to have collaborated in a book about the game, Manoury's *Le Jeu de Dames à la Polonaise*.

As an Englishman, I add with regret the fact that the first international draughts match between England and Scotland in 1884 ended with so decisive a Scottish victory that the matches were not resumed for ten years.

CHAPTER EIGHT

From Cock-Fighting to Football

*Football·'Beastly fury and extreme violence'·Rugger and soccer;
country and town·Florentine football in 1530·'Throwing at cocks'·
Cock-fighting·Boxing·Country games in the seventeenth century·
Jousts and quintains*

WHO invented football? Probably nobody; it just
grew. I have already suggested that, as soon as
man learned to walk erect, he began to kick things
about. To the English, however, goes most of the
credit; they first laid down a code of rules for 'soccer',
and an English school started a new game in 1823 by
breaking such rules as had been laid down—a tablet in
Rugby School close records the fact that 'William Webb
Ellis . . . with a fine disregard for the rules of football as
played in his time, first took the ball in his arms and ran
with it, thus originating the distinctive feature of the
Rugby Game'.

But even William Webb Ellis (who was, I believe, an
Irishman) was less of an innovator than the tablet
would suggest. Gaelic football, first mentioned in public
records in 1600 or thereabouts, allowed players to carry
the ball. At a very much earlier date, the Romans were
playing a game called *harpastum* from which our football
is generally considered to originate; this seems to have
been nearer rugger than soccer. *Harpastum* was almost
certainly played by Roman legionaries during their
occupation of Britain. Some kind of football existed
among the Maoris, the Polynesians, the Eskimos, the
Faroe Islanders and other peoples. And most Italians
would, I think, claim that their *calcio* predated our
football.

However, the name 'football', and most of the terms used in it, are indisputably English and have been adopted all over the world. The British drew up rules so that it ceased to be what Sir Thomas Elyot had called in 1531 'nothing but beastely fury and extreme violence, whereof proceedeth hurte and consequently rancour and malice to remayne with thym that be wounded, wherefor it is to be put in perpetual silence'. Thanks above all to the British, it is no longer 'a develishe pastime . . . and hereof groweth envy, rancour and malice, and sometimes brawling, murther, homicide and great effusion of blood'. Or, to be more accurate, it does not often deserve this definition of it, given by Philip Stubbes in his *Anatomie of Abuses* in 1583.

The first reference in English to the game seems to be in a twelfth-century manuscript, Fitzstephen's *Survey of London*, where there is a reference to *ludum pilae celebrem* which was played all over Britain on Shrove Tuesdays. (True, the 'celebrated ball game' is not there specified as football, but for so many subsequent generations the Shrove Tuesday game was undoubtedly a form of football that Fitzstephen was almost certainly referring to this particular game.)

There is a legend that the first 'football' used in Chester was the head of a Dane. Be that as it may, there is no doubt that the game was often very violent and cruel. It was played by an indefinite number of players on either side and, there being no fast, wheeled traffic such as provides so strong an argument for more playing fields in our day, scores of beefy young men rushed to and fro in the narrow streets. They must have been a pest and a danger to unfortunate pedestrians going about their lawful business. In 1634, the playwright Sir William D'Avenant, pretending to be a Frenchman, wrote sarcastically of the footballers in the main streets of London: 'I would now make a safe retreat, but that methinks I am stopped by one of your heroic games, called football; which I conceive, under your favour, not very conveniently civil in the streets; especially in such irregular and narrow roads as Crooked-lane. Yet it argues your courage, much like your military pastime of throwing at cocks. But your mettle would be more magnified (since you have long allowed these two valiant exercises in the streets) to draw your archers from Finsbury and, during high market, let them shoot at butts in Cheapside.'

Football thus became associated with the worst sort of rowdyism, and, from the fourteenth century onwards it was banned, not only – as with so many other games – because it interfered with training in archery, but also because it led to the loss of so many lives. An exception was made in the case of Ireland – the statutes of Galway in 1527 put an end to all games that might keep men away from their bows and arrows save 'onely for the great foot balle'. Here and there traditional football matches were still played, but by the first half of the nineteenth century it had almost disappeared except in schools rich enough to have their own playing fields. This advantage in richer schools, of course, became more obvious after the development of rugger, for which a relatively soft ground was essential – a low tackle in a cobbled street would have been unpopular, even in a period of 'beastly fury and extreme violence'. One begins to see why rugger came to be the 'snob' game, reserved for the rich or for the dwellers in the country. Soccer could be played after a fashion in almost any dead-end street; rugger could not.

In the absence of proper rules, several varieties of football were played. In East Anglia, for example, there was a game called 'kicking camp' (from the German 'Kampf', or battle?). Several schools besides Rugby and

11(a) Egyptian predecessor of backgammon (p. 145)

11(b) Twelfth-century chessmen, of walrus ivory (p. 78)

12(a) The 'noble and delightsome' sport of cockfighting
(p. 100)

12(b) A form of quintain (p. 104)

12(c) Calcio in Florence: the earliest football? (p. 98)

Eton produced their own forms of football. If Rugby can claim to have originated rugger, Charterhouse, which was then in London and without grass fields for recreation, has a good claim to have originated the practice of 'dribbling', which is so important a feature of soccer.

Many of the larger schools in time adopted rugger as their game, and former pupils of these schools began to form their own clubs. The senior London club, Black-heath, was founded in 1871, and was soon followed by another famous club, Richmond. The English Rugby Union came into existence in 1871; an International Board was formed in 1890. Meanwhile, amateurs of soccer – and they were all amateurs in those days – had formed the Football Association in 1863, and this became the supreme authority throughout the Commonwealth, despite the problems that arose when it was found that thousands of people were prepared to pay to watch expert football for every eleven who were prepared to play it. Inevitably, the amateur made way for the professional, whose financial interests are looked after by the Football League, strongly represented on the Council of the Football Association. The various national associations are affiliated to a body with the clumsy name of *Fédération Internationale de Football Associations*. American football, I must confess, is as incomprehensible to me as English cricket is to most Americans, but it does have certain similarities with rugger.

According to the *Encyclopaedia Britannica*, football 'is essentially a winter pastime, as two requisite conditions for its enjoyment are a cool atmosphere and a soft, firm turf'. Alas for British footballers, this sentence is entirely untrue, as anybody must know who has watched, for example, the Fijian three-quarters sprinting across the *padang* at Singapore with the ground like iron and the temperature well up in the nineties. British football defeats are probably much less due to loss of skill or stamina than to the fact that in other countries football does not have to make way for cricket with the coming of spring. These words are written in Italy on a July Sunday, when the shade temperature in Florence is 95°; tomorrow's newspaper, however, will have practically no news unconnected with football.

Historically, the most famous games of football are those which take place every spring in Florence's Piazza della Signoria. They commemorate the occasion on February 17th, 1530, when the Florentines were being besieged by the armies of the Emperor Charles V, and were very near to starvation. They had been in the habit of celebrating carnival by a football match on the Piazza Santa Croce, near the Arno, and, siege or no siege, they were determined to remain true to their tradition–they played their game with the customary splendour and with trumpeters and drummers placed on the roofs of the neighbouring buildings. Whenever I stand on the Piazzale Michelangelo, whither every foreigner goes to see the stupendous view of Florence, I wonder about the feelings of Charles's mercenaries as they stood on this hill and watched the feigned rejoicings of their enemies just across the river.

Three football games–one on the last Sunday in May in the Boboli Gardens and two in June on the Piazza della Signoria–are still played every year by teams dressed in mediaeval costumes. Each team has twenty-seven players–five men on each wing and the fastest five in the middle; five backs, four three-quarters and three full backs. Their game lasts for fifty minutes on a 'field' a little smaller than a normal soccer ground, and nothing could be less like the *Encyclopaedia's* 'soft, firm turf' than the stone paving of the Piazza della Signoria. The winning team is rewarded by the gift of a fat heifer, in memory of the hungry teams which defied their enemy during the siege of 1530.

*   *   *

The Frenchman whose sarcastic reference to the British 'military pastime' of throwing at cocks was, presumably, a mythical individual created by Sir William D'Avenant. But the criticism was well-founded. In *The Spectator* of February 16th, 1709, Sir Richard Steele wrote that several French writers had commented on British 'throwing at cocks' and other baiting of animals, 'much to our disadvantage', and had imputed this passion to 'a natural fierceness and cruelty of temper'. 'Throwing at cocks' was considered a good and fair sport by both Henry VIII and James I, and men and boys took pride in their skill in throwing sticks at tethered birds until well on in the eighteenth century. On the other hand, fox-hunting, which causes the raising of many a Continental eyebrow today, does not seem to have had very passionate supporters. In the middle of the seventeenth century, for example, a professional fox-exterminator was employed at Sidbury, in south Devon, and church-wardens paid for each fox's head brought to them to be nailed up on the church door. Doubtless foxes were then far more plentiful but one cannot easily imagine a parish council in Devonshire employing a professional fox-exterminator today.

Ever since the Norman Conquest, hunting seems to have been a rather exclusive occupation. King John's Forest Charter was relatively generous—it allowed archbishops, bishops, earls or barons who were travelling through a royal forest to kill a deer or two providing they did so either in sight of a forester or after blowing a trumpet to show that they were not poachers. Senior clerics, even on their way to attend some religious ceremony, often travelled with hawks and hounds, as did Thomas à Becket, for example, during a visit to the French court on behalf of Henry II. When one of the Norman kings went hunting, the sheriff of the county had to provide stabling and carts to take away the shot game. The foresters had to erect 'hides', covered with green branches; in these, the king and his guests waited while huntsmen and hounds drove the game past them, to be shot, shot at, or chased by greyhounds. An un-authorised dog caught in a royal forest had a claw cut from its foot unless the owner hastened to pay a fine on its behalf.

'Cocking' or cock-fighting, has, of course lasted much longer than 'throwing at cocks'. It was known to the ancient Greeks, Persians, Chinese, Indians and Romans. It is still known in many countries, including, I am assured, Great Britain, where it has been considered a sport since the twelfth century. Personally, the only cock-fighting I have seen was at a village market in North Borneo—now Sabah—near the magnificent Mount Kinabalu; the Muruts and other hill aborigines who crowded round the enclosure in a corner of the market place backed their favourites with as much knowledge as did the enthusiasts in Drury Lane or Birdcage Walk in the eighteenth century (as, indeed, was only to be ex-pected, since the original fighting cocks were probably jungle-fowl from South-east Asia). The 'sport' is said to have reached Europe with the help of the Greek soldier and statesman, Themistocles, in the fifth century B.C.; while leading his army against the Persians, he saw two cocks fighting, and stopped his troops so that they could admire, and emulate, the obstinate belligerence of the birds.

The importance attached to cock-fighting is illustrated by the quality of the authors who wrote about it. Gervase Markham, a distinguished poet, wrote a book,

Pleasures of Princes, in 1635, in which he gave detailed advice on 'the Choyce, Ordring, Breeding and Dyeting of the fighting-Cocke for Battell'. He claimed that 'there is no pleasure more noble, delightsome, or void of cozenage and deceipt than the pleasure of Cockynge'. forty years later another poet, Charles Cotton, published his *Compleat Gamester*, in which he claimed that 'cocking is a sport or pastime so full of delight and pleasure that I know not any game in that respect is to be preferred before it, and since the Fighting Cock hath gain'd such an estimation among the Gentry in respect to this noble recreation I shall here propose it before all the other games of which I Have afore succinctly discoursed'.

Markham advised that, before a fight, a cock should be given only fine, white bread and spring water for three or four days. After sparring matches with another cock, in which the spurs of both birds should be padded so that they could not hurt each other, the would-be champion should be put in a basket covered with hay and set to sweat near a fire 'for the nature of this scowring is to bring away his grease, and to breed breath and strength'. Cotton's advice was different and more detailed. The birds, he claimed, should be given 'white sugar-candy, chopt rosemary and butter mingled and incorporated together', after which they should be put in deep straw to make them sweat. 'Towards four or five a clock in the evening take them out of their stoves, and having lickt their eyes and head with your tongue, put them into their pens, and having filled their troughs with square-cut manchet (white bread), piss therein, and let them feed while the urine is hot; for this will cause the scouring to work, and will wonderfully cleanse both head and body.'

For nearly seven centuries, cocking was very popular in schools. In many of them, boys were given a special allowance to buy fighting-cocks, and 'mains', in which several birds fought until there was only one survivor, were always held on Shrove Tuesdays. Parents were expected to pay 'cockpence' on this occasion, and the masters encouraged the event, since their perquisites included the dead birds. Kindness to animals has not always been a British trait. The citizens of Lewes, Sussex, used to celebrate November 5th by burning cats in baskets. John Evelyn, in his diary written in the latter half of the seventeenth century, describes a revolting 'sport' of horse-baiting, which ended when the poor beast had been stabbed to death by knives. Bear-baiting was checked by the Puritans when they took the drastic step of having all the bears killed—there were two famous bear-baiting pits near Shakespeare's Globe Theatre, between Southwark and Blackfriars. Boxing, which became popular early in the eighteenth century as an exceptionally good outlet for gamblers, at least had the merit that the contestants were there of their own free will. I quote, from *Knight's London*, one example of the bombastic style in which one boxer would challenge another in the newspapers.

'Whereas I, William Willis, commonly called by the name of the fighting Quaker, have fought Mr Smallwood about twelve months since, and held him the tightest to it, and bruised and battered more than anyone he ever encountered, though I had the ill fortune to be beat by an accidental fall; the said Smallwood, flushed with the success blind Fortune then gave him, and the weak attempts of a few vain Irishmen and boys, that have of late fought him for a minute or two, makes him think himself unconquerable; to convince him of the falsity of which I invite him to fight me for one hundred pounds, at the time and place above mentioned, when I doubt not I shall prove the truth of what I have asserted by pegs, darts, hard blows, falls and cross-buttocks.' (William Willis lost his fight and his backers lost their money.)

* * *

The more one reads about ancient pastimes, the more one is impressed by the ingenuity with which people, especially in rural areas, kept themselves entertained, despite the long, dark evenings and the absence of such modern-day 'necessities' as broadcasting and television. They had, of course, much less leisure than do people today, but they provided themselves with a fascinating variety of amusements. Burton's *Anatomy of Melancholy*, published in 1621, gave this list of rural recreations: 'Ringing, bowling, shooting, playing with keel-pins, tronks, coits, pitching of bars, hurling, wrestling, leaping, running, fencing, mustering, swimming, playing with wasters, foils, foot-balls, balowns, running at the quintain.' Amusements for 'greater men' included 'riding of great horses, running at rings, tilts and tournaments, horse-races and wild goose chases'. Indoor pastimes included 'cards, tables, dice, shovel-board, chess-play, the philosopher's game, small trunks, shuttlecock, billiards, music, masks, singing, dancing, ule-games, frolicks, jests, riddles, catches, cross-purposes, questions and commands, merry tales of errant knights, queens, lovers, lords, ladies, giants, dwarfs, thieves, cheaters, witches, fairies, goblins and friars'.

Since this book is not an encyclopaedia of pastimes, I need not deal with most of these forms of entertainment. But perhaps a little explanation is needed. A 'waster' was a wooden foil or singlestick. 'Small trunks' was a form of bagatelle, also known as *'trou-madame'*, which I mention elsewhere. No explanation I have found of 'mustering' sounds in the slightest degree entertaining. 'Shovel-board' was a large-scale variety of that splendid public house game, shove ha'penny, of which more in a later chapter. A 'wild goose chase' was not, as its name suggests, the pursuit of a bird, but a kind of horse race in which riders had to follow the exact line taken by the leader. (This must have been more difficult than it sounds, since, to us today, it denotes a vain or hopeless quest.)

The only other occupation in Burton's list which seems to me to call for further comment is 'running at the quintain', since it may be seen to this day by the fortunate visitor to Italy. Like Molière's M. Jourdain, who spoke prose without knowing it, the army recruit who lunges with a fixed bayonet at a sack of straw tied up to look a little like a man might be surprised to learn that he was 'running at the quintain'.

In Arezzo, Foligno, Ascoli Piceno, Udine and the little town of Sarteano, competitors on horseback ride full tilt at a wooden figure known as the 'Saracen' and try with their lances to hit the bull's eye on the target the figure holds.* In most cases, a poor shot causes the 'Saracen's' arm to swing round and to give the unsuccessful competitor a whack on the back. (In the joust at Arezzo, the 'Saracen' does this with a flail to which are attached three balls of lead.) In Pistoia, the procedure is much the same except that the target is held by a wooden bear. In Faenza, the wooden figure is supposed to represent not a Moslem, or 'Saracen', such as was used for the training of crusaders, but an even earlier enemy, namely Hannibal–'Niballo' to the local population. The competitors, dressed generally in fourteenth-century costumes, may look out of place against a background of foreign tourists' cars, but not against the Renaissance buildings surrounding them, and the tradition of the *Quintana*, with varying targets, dates back to Roman times.

* *Gli Antichi Sports e i Giuochi Popolari* (Arezzo, 1966)

'Water quintains' were at one time very popular in England. A pole with a target attached to it was fixed in the river bed, and the competitor whose lance missed its mark lost his balance and fell into the water. Land quintains were very similar to those still practised in Italy—a bad aim at the target caused it to swing round very sharply, and a sandbag attached to it might knock the competitor off his horse unless he was riding at full tilt. At one such quintain, held by Londoners in the presence of King Henry III and his court, the king's servants behaved so badly that the Londoners beat them up, whereupon the king fined London a thousand marks—less on account of their disorderliness than on account of their reluctance to take part in yet another of the crusades.

For a time in England the ordinary pastime of 'running at the quintain' became less fashionable than a kind of tournament in which canes were used instead of lances. For this, the blame or credit goes to King Richard I. According to Strutt,* Richard was at Messina, on his way to the crusades, and he met a Sicilian peasant with a load of canes on his donkey. He and his friends each took a cane, and tilted at each other. Richard's particular opponent was a high-ranking French knight, William de Barres, who had the misfortune to tear the king's hood with his impromptu lance. Richard took this badly, and he charged again at the Frenchman, but his saddle slipped, and he fell to the ground. He charged again, but failed to unhorse the Frenchman, even though Robert de Breteuil, newly created Earl of Leicester, tried to pull the unfortunate William off his horse. Richard appears by now to have been in a thoroughly bad temper. He told Leicester, in what is often called 'no uncertain terms' to mind his own

* Op. cit.

105

business and he told William de Barres never again to appear in his presence. It took the King of France quite a time to bring about a reconciliation.

CHAPTER NINE

Card Games and Origins

Playing cards · Naibi · The origin of cards · Gipsy fortune-tellers · Pin money · Card games throughout the centuries · Bridge · The Goat and Compasses

THE most interesting book about playing cards which has come my way was written by an English clergyman, the Rev. E. S. Taylor.* But as it contains 529 pages and was published more than a century ago, the chances are that it is not one of your bedside books. There have been many others dealing with the history of cards, which is almost as complicated and as confusing as that of chess. As with chess, this history begins somewhere in Asia.

But where? A specific claim is put forward in favour of China—according to a Chinese encyclopaedia published in 1678, cards were invented in A.D. 1120, during the reign of the Emperor Seun-Ho to keep his concubines happy when he was tired. Another story is that they were invented by an Indian matron to stop her husband from pulling out the hairs of his beard. Claims—duller ones—have been put forward on behalf of the Egyptians and the Arabs.

How and when cards came to Europe is a subject of more reasonable, but more vehement, discussion. They must have been well-known in Spain before 1387, for in that year King John of Castile found it advisable to forbid his people to play with them. A British claim is based upon the fact that, before he came to the throne in 1272, Edward I had spent over a year as a crusader in

* *The History of Playing Cards* (John Camden Hotten, London, 1865)

Acre, and a document written a century later referred to a game called the Four Kings. But there seems to be no evidence that this game was played with cards or that Edward had brought back the knowledge of it from his travels. In 1397, a French edict forbad the use of playing cards by poor people. In 1377, the *Consiglio del Capitano*, a kind of city council in Viterbo, discussed the advisability of banning 'a certain game called *naibbe*, which has recently appeared in these parts'. *Naibbe*, later *naibi*, was the name by which cards were at first known in Italy. In his *Storia della Letteratura Italiana*, a Jesuit historian, Gerolamo Tiraboschi, wrote about a manuscript of 1299 which referred specifically to playing cards, but he was writing in the eighteenth century about the thirteenth, and his claim therefore does not carry much conviction.

In 1379, the reigning Prince of Brabant paid 'four peters and two florins, worth eight and a half moutons d'or' for a pack of cards. A German document dated 1380 mentioned the manufacture of playing cards in Nuremberg. And lastly, in 1392, the mad French king, Charles VI, whose passionate interest in tennis I have mentioned in an earlier chapter, received three packs of cards, painted by an artist called Jacquemin Gringonneur, 'for his amusement during the intervals in his sad illness'. It is therefore obvious that card-playing was fairly widespread in Western Europe before the end of the fourteenth century, although the first specific reference to cards in England seems to date from 1463, when card-makers appealed to the government for protection against foreign imports.

But how did they reach Europe in the first place? I have come across four theories. They might have been brought back from the Holy Land by some crusaders who were not devoting all their attention to the capture of the Holy Places from the Moslems. They may have been brought to Spain by the Moorish invaders, who occupied the southern part of that country roughly from the eighth to the fifteenth centuries. They may have reached Italy through the Arabs, or 'Saracens', who occupied Sicily and part of the Italian mainland from the ninth century onwards, or through Greek refugees from Constantinople (which seems unlikely, since the great influx of Greeks to Italy took place only after the Turks had captured that city in 1453). Lastly, cards might have come to Western Europe with the gipsies–a people of Asiatic origin–when they trekked westwards across the Danubian plain.

One guess is nearly as good as another. Quite possibly two or more are correct. For example, the present Spanish name and the former Italian one for playing cards are almost identical–*naipes* in Spanish and *naibi* in Italian–and both names are derived from the Arabic. Thus Moors and Saracens may have introduced cards at roughly the same time into their respective areas of Europe. There seems to be no evidence in favour of the crusader theory. One point in favour of the gipsy theory, on the other hand, is that the earliest cards were almost certainly used rather for occult and mystical purposes than for keeping people amused or for enabling them to win other people's money, and gipsy methods of telling fortunes have a great deal in common with these early cards. But a claim that these gipsies introduced cards to Western Europe by way of Germany is not very convincing, since the first record of the arrival of gipsies in Germany is dated 1414, more than a generation after John of Castile had banned the use of cards in Spain.

There is general agreement that cards were invented in Asia, and that probably the country of their origin was India. Until after the fifteenth century, European playing cards had no queen; nor did cards have a queen in India. In India, the king was supported by a prime minister, or vizier; in early Spanish, Italian and French packs, the court cards were king, *chevalier* and valet, or knave; in Germany, they were king, *ober*, or chief officer, and *unter*, or subaltern. It seems to me significant that in many old packs the *chevalier* or *ober* looks more like a statesman or vizier than like a soldier.

The Italians were probably the first to add a queen to their packs and this, for a time, gave them fifty-six cards—four suits, each of ten 'pip' cards and sixteen 'court' cards (which should really be called 'coat' cards, apparently because they all were persons wearing coats, in contradistinction to the devices of flowers or animals on the other cards of the period). In France, England and some other countries, with the advent of the queen the *chevalier* disappeared altogether.

An additional reason for believing that cards originated in India is supplied by the emblems of the different suits. Why hearts, clubs, spades and diamonds? Why, in Germany, hearts, bells, green leaves and acorns? There must be some reason for these unexpected emblems. They are, in fact, inherited from tarots, the first cards to reach Europe, a full pack of which consisted of seventy-eight cards. In the Spanish and Italian packs, the suits were represented by cups, swords, coins (or rings) and batons (or clubs), and these four emblems are shown in the four hands of the Indian deity, Andhanari. They are said to represent the four classes into which any community could be divided—cups (or chalices) represented the priests; swords represented the armed forces; coins or rings represented the merchants; batons or clubs represented the workers. In Germany, even more obliquely, hearts represented the priests; bells represented the nobility; green leaves represented the landowners; acorns represented the labourers.

It would seem that the English mistranslated the Spanish *espadas*, or swords, into spades. This is certainly no tribute to their knowledge of languages, but it has a certain historical significance – it suggests that Spanish cards may have reached England earlier than French ones, and there is a theory that they were introduced by Eleanor of Castile, who married King Edward I in 1254. If that theory were correct, it would put the British among the pioneers of card-playing. However, like so many theories, it cannot be proved or disproved; I do no more than mention it in passing.

All these cards came originally from packs of tarots, and I have already recorded that a full tarot pack consisted of seventy-eight cards. There were the four suits of ten 'pip' cards and four 'coat' cards, as we know them today (of which one, the *chevalier*, was soon replaced by a queen in Italy, Britain, France and several other countries). There were also twenty-one extraordinary cards known as *'atouts'* and one joker. And the nature of these *'atouts'* helps one to realise that cards were not used originally merely to keep people amused. Here are some of them: the emperor, the pope, the high priestess (in slightly more modern packs, often represented as the mythical Pope Joan), the lovers, the last judgement, the sun, the moon, the hermit, the chariot, the wheel of fortune, the man hanged by one leg, the thunderbolt, the world, the devil, and death (death being the thirteenth *atout*). The pip cards were also decorated with mythical and occult scenes and 'were doubtless employed rather for the fancied interpretation of the will of the unseen God than for the amusement of the profane'.*

As long as gipsies have been known, they have told fortunes, using tarot cards. The earliest book dealing

* E. S. Taylor, op. cit.

with the use of cards for this purpose was printed in Venice in 1540—*Le Sorti*, by Francesco Marcolini—and to the tarots in use at that period, gipsies have since added further cards, so that fairly modern packs contain a fantastic jumble of names, designed to impress their customers. Taylor mentions a pack made in England in the second half of the seventeenth century, and I list some of the persons, historical or fictional, who figure in it: Zoroaster, Friar Bacon, Semiramis, Ptolemy, Copernicus, Dr Faust, Mahommed, Clytemnestra, Nostradamus, Pharaoh, Averroes, Wat Tyler and one or two imaginary saints. (The names of Mahommed, Pharaoh, Nostradamus, Semiramis and Averroes might, perhaps, be taken as evidence of the Asiatic origin of cards; that of Wat Tyler might be taken as a reminder of the chicanery of it all.)

It would seem, then, that from their inception cards have been used for occult purposes by the witch doctors and soothsayers. Tarot games are played anti-clockwise, which superstition holds to be unlucky—one more link with gipsy lore? It seems reasonable to suppose that, if the cards were brought to Europe by the Arabs or even by the gipsies, they may originally have been used to encourage Mahommedanism or some other eastern faith; a French pack from the early fifteenth century has a Saracen as its king of diamonds. So it may be that for this reason, as well as for the more obvious one of discouraging betting, the Christian church at one time strongly opposed card-playing, for subsequently it went out of its way to counter any such heresy by encouraging the use of cards with Christian emblems on them, and with the 'pip' cards representing the various conditions of life, rising with the number of pips to 'faith' and 'theology'.

*　　　*　　　*

13(a) Whist: silence and reflection (p. 121)

13(b) The 'neat and cleanly' game of billiards (p. 131)

14(a) The game of trou madame? (p. 128)

14(b) Skittles, without beer (p. 126)

None of this suggests the use of cards made by you or me. The only people who have inherited memories of the significance of tarots seem to be the gipsies, who produce their grubby packs with which to tell you to expect a letter or to avoid a tall dark man. Tarots are, in fact, still used in parts of southern Europe, but they appear to have lost their mystical significance.

By 1397, tarot cards were sufficiently popular in Paris to necessitate the publication of an order forbidding workmen to play with them on week-days. It was not until the middle of the next century that the French produced the simplified packs as we know them—four suits, each with ten 'pip' cards, and a king, a queen and a knave. The cards were still decorated with all kinds of designs which made it difficult to distinguish their value. Some were educational, and were designed to teach history, geography, astronomy and so on. Others were political; during the French Revolution, the kings, queens and knaves were hurriedly scrapped. Such men as Molière, Rousseau, Voltaire and La Fontaine replaced the kings; such virtues as prudence and justice replaced the queens; Horatius, Hannibal and other great figures of the past replaced the knaves. Otherwise, since the eighteenth century, the French court cards have cele-brated the memory of a strange assortment of historical or mythological figures—David, Caesar, Juno, Minerva, Rachel, Judith, Hector and Lancelot. English cards were almost as strange; they celebrated such events as the downfall of Titus Oates, the defeat of the Spanish Armada, the collapse of the Monmouth rebellion and the bursting of the South Sea Bubble.

The earliest cards—made principally for rich and im-portant people—were often very elegant. They were, of course, hand-painted. Some were engraved on strips of silver or stamped on leather. Louis XVI had some which were engraved on mother-of-pearl. One of the Malatestas, lords of Rimini during the Renaissance, had a pack made of gold, decorated with blue enamel, and Filippo Maria Visconti, Duke of Milan at the same period, paid five hundred gold crowns for a pack. In much more recent and less ostentatious days—in 1880, to be exact—a five of diamonds was sold for £2,750, but only because Holbein had drawn on it a portrait of the Duchess of Norfolk.

I am not sure when playing cards reached the American continent, but one of the companions of Hernan Cortez, conqueror of Mexico in 1519, wrote home about the keen interest shown by the Aztecs in Spanish card games. It is also recorded that Spaniards settled by Columbus on the island of Santo Domingo were reduced to making a pack out of the leaves of a tree.

In the fifteenth century, the invention of engraving on wood and copper made the manufacture of cards relatively easy, and the Germans, in particular, exported them in large quantities. As already mentioned, in 1463, at the urgent request of English makers, the import of foreign cards into England was forbidden. This date is interesting, for Caxton printed his first book in England in 1477, and this gives some weight to the claim put forward by Joseph Strutt that the printing of playing cards from wood blocks preceded the printing of books, or, in other words, that the desire to gamble stimulated and encouraged the desire for knowledge.

English cards at different times have been called 'pairs' (from the Italian, 'un paio', which is here used as a collective noun), 'sets', or 'decks'. And thus I find the answer to one of the questions I asked myself in the first chapter—when the Americans speak of a 'deck' of cards, they are using, as they so often do, an English word dating from the time of Shakespeare which the English themselves have forgotten. The king on British cards is supposed to represent Henry VIII and the queen to be his mother, Elizabeth of York. The knave or valet were not then words used in a derogatory sense – 'knave' presumably came from the German *'Knabe'*, a boy, and a 'valet' was a young man of good family who had not yet achieved knighthood. Ever since Shakespeare's sixteenth century, this card has also been known as a 'jack', and it has been suggested that, since *naipes* was, and still is, the Spanish name for playing cards, a 'jackanapes' is none other than a 'buffoon dressed in bright colours like a knave of cards'. 'Jackanapes' was also a name commonly given to the tame apes that were so fashionable in the sixteenth and seventeenth centuries, but that fact does not necessarily invalidate the suggested derivation of the word.

Since mankind, or a considerable section of it, has a passion for gambling and cards provide excellent opportunities for doing so, it was not long before the authorities clamped down on their use. I have already mentioned John of Castile's attempt to do so in 1387. In England, Henry VII forbad the use of cards, as well as of most other games, by servants and apprentices except during the twelve days of Christmas. He, however, was less worried about their morals than about their archery. Henry VIII was more explicit – everyone between the ages of eleven and sixty, except justices and clergymen, had to practise periodically with the long bow and to keep bows and arrows ready for use (as the Swiss keep their rifles in readiness to this day). 'And none artificer or handy craftsman, husbandman, apprentyce, labourer, servant at husbandry, iorneyman or servant of artificer, maryner, fysherman, waterman or serving man shall play at tables, tennis, dyce, cards, bowles, closh, coyting, logating &c' except at Christmas.

All these restrictions, then, applied only to the 'lower classes'. For his own gambling on Christmas night, Henry VII took with him 'thirty-five unicornis, eleven

French crowns, a ducat, a ridare, and a leu', all of which amounted to the value of £42. Henry VIII, of course, showed a characteristic enthusiasm for gambling. Elizabeth was a keen card-player, but a bad loser. James I gambled a great deal, but was often so lazy that someone else had to hold his cards for him.

Governments of old had to face the same struggle of conscience as do governments of today – gambling may be bad for the morals of the people, but it brings in a useful revenue. Ever since 1712, one card in every British pack has been stamped for excise purposes 'on the spotted or printed side'. As you will see from your own packs, the card selected for this purpose is the ace of spades, and in the eighteenth century there was such a traffic in forged aces that an act was passed in 1756 which made it a felony to forge them. The number of manufacturers was also strictly limited, and to make control easier, none was allowed outside the City of London, Westminster and Dublin. The aces were printed at Somerset House, where the manufacturers had to collect them to complete their packs. The excise duty – threepence a pack since 1862 – had previously fluctuated between sixpence and half-a-crown.

It was not only in Britain that measures were taken to check public gambling while the rulers themselves gambled away large fortunes. During the third crusade, in 1189, King Richard of England and King Philip of France found it necessary to forbid any crusader below the rank of knight to play any game for money. Knights and priests were allowed to play for not more than twenty shillings in twenty-four hours, under penalty of a fine of a hundred shillings, payable to the army's archbishop.

Henry IV of France contracted heavy debts while playing *hazard*, the game from which the Americans are said to have derived craps. Cardinal Mazarin, prime minister to Louis XIV, was one of the greatest gamblers in history, and he gambled even on his deathbed, when he was too weak to hold his own cards. In winter in the Palace of Versailles, there was a gambling session every evening from six o'clock until ten. It was preceded by a concert, to which nobody listened, and the moment the musicians began to pack up their instruments there was a rush to the card tables which seems to have been as undignified and as indecorous as the rush of guests at a Buckingham Palace garden party when the time comes for strawberries and cream in the tea tent.

One more attempt to check gambling seems to me to be worthy of mention. In 1436, Duke Amadeus of Savoy decreed that his subjects might play certain games, providing they did so only for meat and drink. They could play cards as long as the stakes were only pins – *dum ludus fiat tantum cum spinulis* – which Chatto* takes to mean that they might play for trifling sums. Does this explain the expression, 'pin money' – the annual allowance to a woman for her personal expenses on dress and so on? This expression has been current in Britain since the sixteenth century; until recent times pins were very expensive, and it is recorded that the Roman emperor, Caligula, 'gave 100,000 *sesterces* to his Curtisan to buy her pins'.

*   *   *

The other day I read somewhere that Louis XV and Madame du Barry were very fond of playing *vingt-et-un*, which was also one of Napoleon's favourite card games. And I find myself back in a billet just south of Ypres in April 1915 – a shabby little *estaminet* with half a dozen officers asleep on palliasses along one wall, and another half dozen, of whom I am one, sitting round a table

* *Facts and Speculations on the Origin and History of Playing Cards* (Russell Smith, London, 1848)

playing *vingt-et-un*. I am banker, and am winning more than I have ever won before, when someone announces that we have to move up the line to the trenches again in a quarter of an hour. A little dramatically, I order two bottles of champagne—the first bottles I have ever ordered—and we snatch drinks in moments between jamming this or that article into our packs. As we trudge along the muddy road towards the communicating trench, I am suddenly poignantly aware of the beauty of the sunset and its red light on the splintered trees, aware that even this shattered and devastated world is incredibly lovely. We reach the zone where the first German stray bullets plop into the untilled earth near us. Isn't it unlucky, I ask myself, to win at cards? And I find it very difficult to hide the fact that I am filled with fear. . . .

That must have been a few days before the Second Battle of Ypres and the first German gas attacks. On that occasion winning at cards does not seem to have brought me bad luck—within forty-eight hours, a very slight wound sent me back to hospital in Rouen; within sixty hours, most of my friends in the regiment had been gassed, wounded or killed. I went back to Ypres some years ago, and there were their names, recorded on neat little tombstones, near the summit of Hill 60.

*　　*　　*

A few paragraphs about some of the card games. One of the oldest was the Spanish game of *primero*, played, of course, with tarot cards, with their twenty-two *atouts*, a word which the French have retained as their word for trumps. The English word, 'trumps' probably comes from the seventeenth-century game which, in turn, came from the French game called *triomphe*. Primero led on to the Spanish game of *hombre* which, without the 'h', became immensely popular in England and France in the seventeenth century. *The Court Gamester*, a book published in 1720 for the guidance of the daughters of the future George II, pointed out that the game 'has a great deal of the gravity peculiar to that nation [Spain]' and that it called for 'a great deal of application'—enough to turn any normally lively young girls against it. Several other books refer to the 'absolute silence' in which it was played. Nevertheless, the young princesses were assured that 'it will be found the most delightful and entertaining of all games to those who have anything in them of what we call the spirit of play'.

Hoc Mazarin was another Spanish game introduced into France and modified slightly by Cardinal Mazarin. It was banned by the Vatican and also by the French government, but the cardinal seems serenely to have continued to use it as a vehicle for his passion for gambling. *Bouillotte* had some resemblance to poker, and also to an Italian game, *frusso*, which was played some five centuries ago, to *primero* and to another French game, *ambigu*. *Ambigu* is dismissed in the *Encyclopédie Larousse* as 'a kind of card game which is no more than a combination of several other games—whist, *bouillotte* etc'. I look up *bouillotte*, and read that it is a form of *brelan*. I look up *brelan*, and am assured it was a game only very remotely related to poker. And here I give up the search.

Some experts trace the lineage of poker to much earlier times. It descends, they say, from a Persian game called *as ras*, which is also the ancestor of gleek, to which I shall come in a paragraph or two. Aveline, in *Le Code des Jeux*, says the name merely means that it is a game designed to stir up one's opponents. A more probable explanation is that it is an Anglo-Saxon mispronunciation of the French *poque*, which was yet one more obsolete game. If the game came to North America from France, it is believed to have done so through Louisiana, when that territory was still part of the French empire, and it was tremendously popular on the old Mississippi paddle-wheel steamers nearly a century and a half ago.

An early mention of poker in America is in a book published in 1843 and entitled *Exposure of the Arts and Miseries of Gambling*, a title which somehow has failed to divert players to less miserable activities. In early days a buck-horn knife on the table showed who was the dealer, and apparently this is the origin of 'passing the buck'.

Rummy, also called coon-can, conkin and zum-khum, is said to come from a Spanish game called *conquian* and to have reached the United States rather more than a century ago by way of Mexico. *Barbacolle, commère, accomodez-moi* and *pharaon*—a game to which Marie-Antoinette was devoted—were related to *lansquenet*, which was brought to France in the sixteenth century by the German mercenaries known as *Landsknechte*. Rabelais refers to the game in *Gargantua*, published in 1542. *Baccara*, well-known to frequenters of casinos, was introduced to France by soldiers of King Charles VIII, returning from his Italian campaign which brought him as far as Naples in 1495. *Piquet* was another game mentioned by Rabelais and was played in England, under the name of *cent* or *sant*, from 1550 onwards. Gleek, mentioned above, is said to get its name from the German *Glück*, or good luck, but it, too, was French, and was mentioned by Villon in 1461. Like *ombre* and several other games that were popular in the seventeenth century, it was played by three people, and three-cornered tables were to be found in most well-to-do houses. Catherine of Aragon, the first wife of Henry VIII, was an enthusiastic player. The ace was known as Tib; the knave was Tom; four was Tiddy; five and six were Tower and Tumbler, and counted double.

Triomphe and another game known as ruff-and-honours were among the games that led on to whist, the name of which has been explained, most unconvincingly, by the fact that, unlike most card games of the time, it called for silence and reflection. (In any case, the name originally was 'whisk', which leaves one just as puzzled.) Whist was probably invented in the seventeenth century, but it became fashionable only in 1730, when Lord Folkestone and some of his friends formed the habit of playing it in the Crown Coffee House in London's Bedford Row. It is one of the few games that the French took over from the English, and the seriousness with which it was played led Horace Walpole to suggest that the French had adapted England's two dullest possessions—whist and the novels of Samuel Richardson. Whether his malice was justified I do not know, for I have neither played the one nor read the other. Voltaire was a keen player, although with some complaints about the difficulty of pronouncing its name. Aveline claims that it was invented 'to give repose to British members of parliament after they had discussed affairs of state throughout the day'. Charles Cotton wrote of whist, with truth and apparently without disapproval, 'He that can by craft overlook his adversary's game hath a great advantage'.

Bridge, of course, is relatively modern, being introduced into various London clubs during the last decade of the last century. Somewhat similar games to it were played in Denmark, Turkey, Russia, Greece, Egypt, Sweden and the United States (where it was called Siberia). Turkey seems to have the best claim to have made it popular, although in England it was at first called 'Biritch or Russian whist'. Boston, another derivative from whist, was invented during the American War of Independence either by Americans in Boston who were being besieged by the British or by officers of the French fleet lying off the near-by port of Marble-head, where two small islands in the harbour are still called Great and Little Misery, corresponding to terms used in the game.

It is thus obvious that, despite their different names, most card games resemble each other and their remote ancestors. Scores have become obsolete, presumably because they were replaced by slightly more captivating variations. But the names of some of them leave one with some regret that they have disappeared. Among the games that once were popular in England were dumb knight, knave out of doors, bone ace, beast, wit and reason, lanterloo, penneech and Queen Nazareen. According to Hoyle,* games in which the entire pack is dealt out to four players, and in which two play as partners against the other two and collect tricks against them are British in origin or adaptation.

*　　*　　*

I have written only about the cards of Western Europe or North America. But if playing cards originated in Asia it would be unfair to make no reference at all to Asian card games.

Indian cards, believed to be the ancestors of them all, are or were generally circular or oblong, and were painted in very vivid colours on paste-board or mother-of-pearl. There were normally ninety-six of them, although for some games the number was increased to a hundred and twenty, and they are remarkable for their similarity to European cards, even in the emblems by which the suits are distinguished. They had a crown, representing the king; silver money, representing the merchants; a slave, representing the workers; and swords, representing the soldiers.

* *Encyclopaedia of Games* (Goren, New York, 1950)

Chinese cards, which are long and narrow—nearly four inches by one—are in packs of thirty or thirty-two. Morley* writes that one Chinese card game has a name identical with that of Chinese chess, and means chariots, horses and guns. (As we have seen in an earlier chapter, chess was looked upon in Asia as a peaceful outlet for the feelings of military men.) Japanese cards differ from all the others, and are notable for their elegance. They have twelve suits, each of only four cards, but one point which they have in common with cards in many other countries is the presence of one card that is 'wild' and represents the joker.

I end this chapter with two paragraphs that have nothing to do with games but that are suggested to me by them. As long ago as 1841, *Knight's London* protested against 'the perversion of the pious old tavern legend of "God encompasseth us" into the sign of "The Goat and Compassess"'. But is it a 'perversion?' In an illustration of a sixteenth-century pack of German cards in Morley's collection there is a goat with a pair of compasses in its mouth. Why compasses in the mouth of a sixteenth-century goat? I can find no satisfactory explanation, for I am unconvinced by the theory that the name may derive from the arms of the Cordwainers' Guild, in which there are three goats' heads with a chevron—not unlike a compass—between them.

Still less am I convinced by the widespread belief that London's famous 'Elephant and Castle' is a corruption of 'The Infanta of Castile'. There were inns bearing that name before the Infanta married into the English royal family. An alternative explanation goes back again to one of the City Companies, in this case to the Company of Cutlers, which imported elephant tusks for their ivory-handled knives. But, in John

* *Old and Curious Playing Cards* by H. T. Morley (Batsford, London, 1931)

Boardman's *Greek Art** there is a photograph of a plate, dating from the third century B.C., which shows a battle elephant with a formidable fortress on its back. Again, Virgil referred to '*elephantus turritus*', or 'towered elephant' as a military weapon. To take one more, and more recent example, in Italy, near Viterbo, there is the deserted Orsini castle of Bomarzo, with a park in which are huge and horrific statues of beasts and giants. Among them is a statue of an elephant, carrying a large castle on its back and crushing a centurion with its trunk. In the chapter on chess, I mentioned the confusion, very early in the history of that game, between the 'elephant', which later became the bishop, and the 'tower' or 'castle', which is now generally known as the 'rook'. No infantryman called upon to face a 'towered elephant' in war would be likely to forget the experience, and even the elephant of today, with a howdah on its back, would be worthy of commemoration on signs swinging outside public houses. So 'Infanta of Castile', no! But how, when and why the 'Elephant and Castle?'

* Thames and Hudson, London, 1964

CHAPTER TEN

Mainly Bowls and Billiards

The ancient game of bowls · Bowls, bowling and skittles · Polo and billiards · Skating and ski-ing · The British style

O F all British outdoor pastimes it is probable that bowls, in one form or another, is second in antiquity only to archery, and archery, as we have seen, was more of a military exercise than a sport. One needs to keep in mind the differences between bowls, bowling and skittles, all of which presumably derive from what William Fitzstephen, writing in the twelfth century, called 'casting of stones' (*'in jactu lapidum'*). In the royal library at Windsor, there is a contemporary drawing of two men throwing at a small cone, instead of a jack, as in bowls today. Certainly, bowls, in a very primitive form, was a very popular pastime in the thirteenth century and perhaps earlier.

With the customary ban, in the interests of better archery, the game degenerated. It was played in the back yards of inns and taverns which, in the days of cheap and vile alcohol, became so disreputable that even now one may hear expressions of disapproval of the few inns that still retain bowling or skittle alleys for the great and harmless pleasure of their customers. 'Common bowling alleys', wrote Stephen Gosson, 'are privy moths that eat up the credit of many idle citizens; whose gains at home are not able to weight down their losses abroad; whose shops are so far from maintaining their play, that their wives and children cry out for bread, and go to bed supperless often in the year.' But Gosson wrote his *School of Abuse* four centuries ago.

These circumstances hastened to mark the distinction

between bowling and bowls, the latter word being first used in England in 1511. Bowling seems to have originated at least six centuries ago in Germany and the Netherlands, and in due course to have been taken to the New World by Dutch emigrants. Their descendants continued to play the game until 1840 near the southern tip of Manhattan Island, where a small area at the end of Broadway is still known as Bowling Green. There are also towns bearing that name in Ohio, Missouri and Kentucky, and it is not surprising that the recent passion for bowling alleys in Europe should have come back across the Atlantic from the United States. But the game, although on a humble scale, is an old one in Britain, and, for a time, was highly respectable; Henry VIII added to his Whitehall Palace 'divers fair tennice courts, bowling alleys and a cockpit'. Where they stood, now stands that greatest opponent of luxury expenditure, the British Treasury.

Bowling alleys were at first made of slate or hardened clay; the smart bowling alleys of today are made of alternating narrow strips of pine and maple. There were nine 'pins'–also called 'skittles', which is misleading, since the game of that name is quite different from bowling–set up on a 'diamond'. Early in the nineteenth century, when the game was forbidden by law, players got round the ban by adding a tenth pin, set up on a triangle.

In skittles, the object is similar to that in bowling–to knock over as many pins as possible. But this is not done with a ball rolled along the ground; instead, the instrument is a flattened, oval 'cheeze', often weighing ten pounds or more, which is thrown underhand. The alley, therefore, is very much shorter than the bowling alley. In very early days, players used either bones or sticks shaped like a policeman's truncheon instead of 'cheezes'. In the remoter areas of South Africa you may, if you are lucky, find the descendants of the Boer farmers playing *Jukskei*, with bottle-shaped pieces of wood, up to eighteen inches long and three in diameter. These heavy implements, copied from part of the yokes of the old ox-wagons, are thrown at a pin fifty-two feet away.

Bowls has, of course, developed into a very different game from bowling or skittles, since it requires very carefully-tended lawns and bowls which are 'biased' so that they will 'draw' about six feet in thirty yards. Also, the aim is not to knock down a set of pins but to leave one's bowl as close as possible to the small target ball, known as the 'jack'. The invention or discovery of 'bias' is an old one; it dates from somewhere about the middle of the sixteenth century, and it may be remembered that Shakespeare made a reference to it in his *Richard II*. Bowls, in common with so many other games, was declared unlawful at different periods, but, rather unexpectedly, John Knox, visiting Calvin in Geneva on a Sunday, found that austere reformer playing bowls, and John Aylmer, a sixteenth-century bishop of London, also played on Sunday afternoons, using language as he did so which 'justly exposed his character to reproach'.

Outside Britain, bowls is a much less scientific game, partly, no doubt, because few countries have a climate which produces such superb turf. But nobody who has joined in a game in a French or Italian village could doubt the skill with which a player takes advantage of every bump in the dusty ground. And the dust provides an excellent excuse for just one more glass of that rough local wine.

To make a good green, the ground must be dug to a depth of eighteen inches, must be well-drained, and must have layers of gravel, ashes, moulds and silver sand spread over it before it is covered by thick turf, preferably from some place near the sea. The resulting green is certainly a very beautiful sight, but some people would prefer the dust, the chipped wooden balls and the local wine in a village in Provence. I am one of them.

There are, of course, many other games associated with bowls and bowling. Kayles (from the French *'quilles'*) was played many centuries ago, with the players throwing a stick at the 'kittle pins', the tallest of which was the 'king pin'. In cloish, a ball was used instead of a stick, but it, too, was thrown, not rolled, and was therefore a form of skittles. In loggats, sheeps' knuckle bones were used instead of sticks or balls, and the target was a long bone. A game called Nine Holes was popular in the early seventeenth century and again at the end of the eighteenth, after skittles had been banned. This game, or another very like it, was also called Bumble Puppy but I don't know why. Small metal balls were thrown or rolled along a smooth floor in which numbered holes were sunk. Small-scale varieties of this are, or were, to be found in every nursery and, under the name of *Boule*, have deprived tourists in Swiss casinos of many thousands of francs.

Very close to Bumble Puppy, and with just as puzzling a name, was *Trou Madame* or Troule in Madame, which was a form of bowls with numbered holes in a board. According to a sixteenth-century document on 'The Benefits of the Ancient Bathes at Buckstone',* the balls used were 'of leade, bigge, little or meane, also of Copper, Tynne, Woode, eyther vyolent or softe, after their owne discretion'. This same document contains a warm recommendation to men to play bowls, since 'the game dothe not only strengthen the stomach and upper parts above mydryfe or wast; but also the middle parts beneath the sharp gristle and

* *Pleasures of the Past* by Iris Brooke (Odhams, London, 1955)

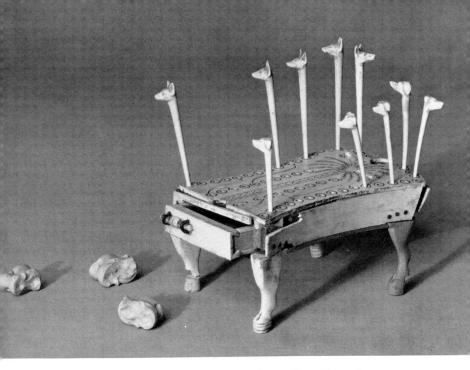

15(a) Dogs and jackals: one of the earliest Egyptian games
(p. 144)

15(b) Chinese playing lin-po, an early board game

16 The ale house: forerunner of the English 'pub' (p. 137)

the extreme parts, as the handes and legges, according to the wayght of the thing trouled, fast, soft or meane'. So now you know.

*   *   *

I must mention two other ball games, of which one requires a very large field and the other a very large room. The former, polo, is of course a game of great antiquity, some authorities claiming that it was played before 500 B.C.; it certainly was played in very early times in Persia, India, China, Japan and Byzantium, the Greek city which stood where Istanbul now stands. The great Maidan square in Isfahan, Persia (now, of course, Iran) is said to have been the world's first polo ground, and goal posts adorn each end of it to this day. The name, however, comes from the Tibetan word for a ball made of willow root—the wood from which polo balls are made. Persia is generally looked upon as the home of polo, and the Persian poet Firdawsi, whose history of his country, written in 60,000 couplets, was finished in the year 1010, describes the first international polo match—between Persia and Turkey. So that a proper code of rules must have been accepted in Asia at about the time when King Canute was trying to check the rising tide in England.

The British polo ground is 300 yards long and 200 wide; the Persian ground was sometimes twice as long. The British goal-posts are made of basket-work or of *papier maché,* so that a collision with one of them is unlikely seriously to damage horse or rider. The Persian game was a very tough one, but a document exists which refers to seventy veiled maidens who rode astride and played polo in Persia at the end of the sixth century.

At different times and in different countries, there have been several variants of the game. The present stick, in most cases, seems to have been preceded by a kind of racket, and the gap between the goal-posts was filled in with boarding, in which there was a hole about a foot in diameter. At the back of this there was a bag of netting, and the player scored a goal by hitting the ball into this net—the Japanese game still retains this feature. The rules under which Persia played Turkey, however, were probably closer to those that obtain today, with the teams ranged up at opposite ends of the field and with the ball hit along the ground, and not being carried on or in a racket. Players of today can use sticks with square or cigar-shaped heads; the latter are generally used by Americans and Indians, but the square stick (in appearance, rather like an elegant, long-handled croquet mallet) is often preferred on soft English grounds.

If one must watch games instead of playing them, there can be very few more exciting to watch and very few pleasanter places in which to watch them than polo in Cowdray Park, under that splendid line of England's South Downs.

*   *   *

The game that calls for a very large room is, of course, billiards which, according to a Major General A. W. Drayson,* writing in 1890, 'possesses advantages over every other game. It can be played by daylight or gaslight, by both sexes, and there is no reason why a lady should not play equally as well as a gentleman; in fact, I have played with a lady who has scored a break of thirty.'

The former prejudice against billiards, he wrote, was due to the fact that 'it was played principally in public houses, and the players were not always those who belonged to the respectable class. These men studied the

* *Handbook of Games* edited by Dr W. Pole (George Bell, London, 1890)

game for the sole purpose of being able to win money from the unwary. The rooms were dirty, and drinking was considered a necessary accompaniment of the game. . . . On joining the Royal Military Academy as a cadet, I found that by the standing orders any cadet known to enter a billiard room was liable to seven days arrest, while at the present time there is a billiard room at the Academy at which cadets may play.' It is the only ball game, someone has pointed out, which is (or was) played by men in evening dress, and in Edwardian days Inman, Tom Newman and other champions played their matches in stiff shirts and white waistcoats.

The gallant Major General had a good deal to say on the etiquette of billiards beyond the obvious warning against moving about the billiard room while a player is preparing his stroke. Spectators, he wrote, should not 'strike a fusee for the purpose of lighting a pipe or cigar'. *The School of Recreation*, published in 1684, and quoted by Iris Brooke,* claimed that billiards encouraged good behaviour and discouraged smoking, since it deterred players from taking up a 'lolling, slovenly posture' and from the 'stinking indecency' of tobacco. 'This pastime being of a neat and cleanly composition will not admit any such irregularities and indecorums.' Billiards, in the opinion of Charles Cotton, writing in the seventeenth century, was a 'gentile, cleanly and most ingenious game'.

Billiards is an old game, even if one rejects the claim—as I think one must—that the Scythian philosopher Anacharsis saw a game very similar to billiards when he was travelling in Greece in 400 B.C. Also it is probably not nearly as old as Shakespeare appeared to believe—in his *Anthony and Cleopatra*, written in 1607, he has Cleopatra, bored by the absence of Anthony, say-

* Op. cit.

ing to her attendant, Charmian, 'let us to billiards', a
game which Charmian avoids with the excuse that 'my
arm is sore'. She was wise to do so; billiards is not a
game to be played merely because one is bored.

Cotton claims, in his *Compleat Gamester*, that billiards
originated in Italy or Spain, but most writers place it in
France, where it has been played since the second half
of the fifteenth century. Some French writers, on the
other hand, ascribe its invention to the English. The
name itself almost certainly comes from the French
bille, which referred to the curved cues in use until the
middle of the seventeenth century, and afterwards to the
balls themselves. (Incidentally, the 'pockets' are known
as '*blouses*' in France; as every visitor to a French *café*
knows, there are nowadays no pockets in a French
billiard table.) Louis XIV (1638–1715) was a keen
player, and was strongly recommended to become one
by his doctor. (The great French encyclopaedia,
Larousse, refers to the game as 'hygienic and amusing'–
adjectives which, with the stale atmosphere and semi-
religious silence of many billiard rooms in my memory,
are not ones I should have selected.) Charles IX of
France is said to have played billiards during the mas-
sacre of the Huguenots on St Bartholomew's Day in 1572.

There have been several varieties of the game, the
most popular of which seems to have had some affilia-
tion with croquet–and, indeed, one very early variety
of billiards was played on grass. In the seventeenth
century, where there is now the 'spot' for the red ball,
there stood an ivory arch nearly twice the width of the
ball. This was called the 'port' or the 'pass'. At the
'baulk' end, or on the middle spot, was an upright pin,
known as the 'king'. The first job was to get through
the 'port'; the second was to hit the 'king' with your
opponent's ball, not your own. Another variety, known
as Mississippi, had, at the far end, a board with several

numbered arches, and one's aim was to hit one's ball through these arches off the cushion. In The Rocks of Sicily—a form of bagatelle—the top of the table was semicircular and raised, and one aimed to get the ball into one or other of the small hollows dotted about the table, despite the diversions caused by nails here and there. Thus people who go in for mild gambling at the pin tables are playing games that have scarcely changed during two centuries.

Originally, the billiard cue was a stick about a yard long and flattened out at one end into a kind of spoon. It was with this butt end that the player hit the ball, and, to do so, he must not touch the table, even with his sleeve. The use of the point of a straight cue, instead of the butt of a curved one—which took place early in the last century—completely changed the game, and all the more so when chalk on the tip of the cue made it possible to put on 'side'. Then came the use of slate beds instead of oak and marble. Rubber formed the cushions after 1835. The game, in fact, became so scientific and the tables so accurate that, learning from American and French players, whose tables have no pockets and who therefore score entirely by cannons, British champions began to knock up scores that took all the excitement out of the game. When, in 1926, Reece scored a break of 1,151, with 568 consecutive cannons, by use of the 'pendulum' stroke, the Billiards Association and Control Council limited consecutive direct cannons to thirty-five. And Reece, in the nineteen-twenties, could not compare with the Australian Lindrum, in the nineteen-thirties.

Billiards on that scale can scarcely be called 'amusing'. On my scale, it can. Many years ago, when the League of Nations was still striving to avoid the second world war, we used to meet, late in the evening, round the French billiard table in Geneva's *Club International*. In the centre of the table we drew a chalk circle of about four inches diameter, and in the middle of it we stood a cork. On the cork each of us put a piece of twenty centimes. If one could knock over the cork with the white ball by a cannon or off the cushion, one pocketed any coins that fell outside the circle. If one had the misfortune to hit the cork with the red ball, one replaced the coins that fell outside. Not billiards, perhaps, but good fun, which helped one to forget the frustrations of the League Assembly.

*   *   *

I add here a few paragraphs about winter sports, mainly because I do not know where else to put them. One thinks of ski-ing, and even of skating, as very modern amusements, but the problem of moving across snow or ice is, of course, one which has worried men in cold climates ever since they killed wild animals for the food and warm skins they provided. Xenophon, whose *Anabasis*, written in the fourth century B.C., has worried many generations of schoolboys, described how Armenian horses were shod with snow-shoes, and snow-shoes, in a great variety of shapes and sizes, have long been in use everywhere near the Arctic Circle, from Mongols to Lapps to Eskimos to North American Indians. Procopius, Byzantine historian in the fifth century, wrote of the Lapps as wearing snow-shoes. In old Norse sagas, the god of winter was described as walking on skis. The first recorded skis were curved frames covered with leather. The Cree Indians had snow-shoes nearly six feet long, and thus came very near to being ski-runners. The Swedish army of Gustavus Adolphus had infantry equipped with skis.

Modern ski-ing – the kind of ski-ing which in winter dots every mountain slope with keen young people in the gayest of colours and links smart hotels to remote peaks by ski-lifts and *téléfériques* – may be said to have originated in the Telemark region of Norway rather more than a century ago. Being a Norwegian word, the 'k' should be pronounced as though it were an 'h', but this pronunciation is generally rejected in France and Switzerland, for reasons that are obvious to French speakers. The telemark of my youth, in sparkling powder snow, has long since given way to the christiania, the kick turn and other alarming ways of checking one's speed or changing one's direction on snow as hard as ice; nevertheless, had I youth, courage and leisure, I should divide my time between ski-ing, surf-riding and gliding.

People have skated on ice for at least eight centuries. The early skates generally consisted of leg bones or jaw bones of horses or cows, and Fitzstephen, in his twelfth-century *Description of London*, explained, with pardonable exaggeration, that 'some tye bones to their feete and under their heeles and shoving themselves with a little picked staffe, doe slide as quicklie as a birde flyeth in the aire or an arrow out of a crosse-bow'.

As the credit for skis goes to the Norwegians, the credit for skates, of course, goes to the Dutch. A French writer in the eighteenth century remarked that Dutch women knitted as they skated along, carrying baskets or jars of milk (on their heads, I presume, unless they had also been clever enough to knit with one hand). The Dutch also produced the first skates with metal blades, in 1600 or thereabouts, and by 1770 they were using roller skates on their roads. Ten years earlier, a certain Joseph Merlin, who had invented a form of roller skate, gave a demonstration at Carlisle House in London; this was memorable chiefly because his skates ran away with him and he smashed into a very valuable mirror. London's first public rink was opened in an old tennis court in Windmill Street, just off Piccadilly Circus, in 1823, and an ice rink, or *glaciarum*, was opened in 1876 in that even more famous street, King's Road, Chelsea.

According to the eleventh edition of the *Encyclopaedia Britannica*, 'in the British style of figure skating, which is not recognised by the International Skating Union, the body is held as nearly as possible upright, the employed leg is kept straight, the unemployed leg carried behind, the arms hang loosely at the side, and the head is turned in the direction of progress. . . . Much more latitude is allowed by the Continental school . . . the knee of the employed leg is slightly bent, and the unemployed leg is in constant action, being used to balance the body during the execution of the figures. The Continental is less difficult in execution than the British style, but its movements are less graceful. . . . The Continental varies from the complete *abandon* of the French to the more restrained style of the Germans.'

What a limitless ocean is the English Channel!

CHAPTER ELEVEN

Games in English Pubs

The English inn · Darts · Solitaire · The devil among the tailors and riots in the Haymarket · Shove ha'penny · Dominoes

ENGLISHMEN are compelled by their climate to spend more time indoors than are most other men, and the 'pub', be it in town or country, is still an institution which promises to survive even in this chrome and plastic age. Copies of the English inn are now to be found in many parts of the world and do quite a lot to raise the exaggeratedly low reputation of English cooking and even of English beer – one no longer hears the advice given to American soldiers on their arrival in Britain during the war, namely that they should pour it back into the horse. No book about games and pastimes should omit the 'pub', the most genuinely democratic institution in the British Isles, despite its public bar, its private bar, its tap room and its saloon bar. Long may it thrive!

The game of darts has, of course, replaced almost all other pub games, although shove-ha'penny boards, carefully polished with beer and elbow grease, are still fairly common. The two world wars sent so many thousands of men away from their homes and into the public houses for their few hours of relaxation and leisure that dart boards are now sometimes found in the most imposing mansions (where they look to me as hopelessly out-of-place as a cupboard full of delicate china would look in a public bar; the dart-board calls for the low ceilings, the mahogany bar, the rows of bottles and the beer levers of a pub).

In this, however, I am probably wrong, for at one

time the game of darts enjoyed high social status. According to a lively adventure in advertising,* it was played in the seventeenth century, and one player was Henry VIII himself—he played so many games that one wonders how he found time to deal with Cardinal Wolsey, Sir Thomas More, and all his wives. Boards used to be made of rolled paper fixed endways on to a wooden board; nowadays, the rolled paper has been replaced by bristles.

Nobody seems to know much about the history of darts, but at least the game was known in the seventeenth century, and by a prisoner in the Bastille. He was a French historian, Paul Pelisson, whose claim to immortality is based less upon his writings than upon his success in taming a spider that shared his cell. Besides this achievement, he managed to procure some long pins, converted them into darts, and used the wooden panelling of his cell as a dartboard.

Here, a short reference to a pastime which is played rather by lonely old people than by roisterers in the public bar, but which is said also to have been invented by a Frenchman who had been 'embastillé', or imprisoned in the Bastille. Solitaire, fairly popular when I was a boy, has for two generations been an almost forgotten game, and the circular boards are now seldom seen outside antique shops. Even the marbles, such as those which filled the fifty holes of our board when I was a small boy, are rarities. I hear that there has been renewed interest in solitaire but it has largely been replaced by a great variety of card games of patience or by one-man scrabble—during one voyage from Singapore I found myself involved in a daily game of scrabble with a widow who, in the ordinary way, had only herself to play against. With so many hours to kill, the more time she

* The Watney Book of Pub Games by Timothy Finn (Queen Anne Press, London, 1967)

could waste on reflection before she made a move, the happier she became. And, try as I would to avoid the forms of 'gamesmanship' I mentioned in my chapter on chess, I could not prevent my impatience from smothering my pity.

A game which one finds far too seldom in public houses is 'devil among the tailors', which the Oxford English Dictionary describes as a game in which a top— the 'devil'—is set spinning down a sloping board to knock down as many ninepins—'tailors'—as possible. *The O.E.D.*, like the proverbial customer, is always right, but the game I know is a very different one. It is a kind of miniature skittles, in which a small wooden ball suspended from a tall pole is aimed at pins set up at the other end of a board, placed on the top of an ordinary pub table. To achieve good results, the player must send the ball off on an elliptical curve as subtle as that obtained in bowls by a proper use of the bias.

I like this game partly because I have played it in such pleasant West of England inns and partly because I am puzzled by its name. The Watney book, mentioned in an earlier paragraph, says that the name comes from a riot of London tailors in 1783. The Theatre Royal in the Haymarket was to put on a benefit performance for an actor named Dowton, and he chose an old play called *The Tailors, or a Tragedy for Warm Weather*. But the tailors of London considered this play was an insult to their trade and threatened a riot if it was staged. Dowton was a tough Devonian who was not easily intimidated, even though the tailors threatened him with death and the theatre with destruction. On the night, the theatre was so packed with shouting tailors that no word of the play could be heard. At one moment, Dowton narrowly escaped being hit by a pair of tailor's shears, and when the mob inside and outside the theatre threatened to burn it down the principal magistrate from Bow Street was sent for. His constables could not restore order, and in the end dragoons had to charge the crowd. The game of table skittles was becoming popular at the time, but I am still curious as to how it came to be connected with a riot in the Haymarket. I appealed to the Stage Director at the theatre, and, besides giving me the above details, he suggested that Dowton's Devonshire origin might have something to do with it, but the Watney book dispels my belief that it is a West Country game; on the contrary, 'it is one of the most universal of English games'. Probably, however, Dowton was the 'devil'.

That shove ha'penny is old, nobody could deny, and it does not deserve its dismissal by Strutt as a game that is 'only practised by such as frequent tap-rooms'. On one occasion, Henry VIII lost £45 to Lord Rockford in a game of 'shoveller bourde', which is one of its many variants. In the sixteenth century almost every large house had a 'shovel-board', which might be as much as thirty feet long, and which was a cross between the 'shove ha'penny' of the village inn and the 'shuffle-board' as played by thousands of ships' passengers, who push wooden discs along the deck with a long pole. In 'shovel-board', as in its miniature variety, 'shove ha'penny', each player tries to get his pieces between the several transverse lines, and to prevent his opponent from doing so. Shove ha'penny proper—the public house variety—is played on a small board of hardwood or slate on a pub table, and its antiquity is indicated by the fact that it was formerly known as 'shove groat' or 'slyp groat'. Yet another of its former names was 'Justice Jarvis', but I do not know why. Say what you will, there is a certain beauty about the gentleness with which some farm labourer with a fist like a sledge-hammer will nudge his coin into the proper 'bed' with the palm of his hand.

The last game to be mentioned in this chapter is still popular in British pubs, but much less so than in the cafés of continental Europe. Many years ago, when I was a lonely student in Madrid, I went for a day excursion to the magnificent city of Segovia. It was very hot, and I walked through the streets for hours, trying to find the courage to enter a café for some food and drink. At last I went down some steps and opened a door leading into a long, low room, so dark in contrast to the hot glare outside that I could at first see nothing at all. And, in this darkness, the voices of invisible men were almost overwhelmed by a strange and alarming rustle, such as might be made by millions of lizards running away through dry and brittle grass. I was so frightened that I was strongly tempted to turn again up the steps into the harsh sunlight.

When at last I could distinguish men, tables, chairs and glasses, I discovered that everyone in the café was playing dominoes, and the sinister noise was being made as they shuffled the 'cards' on the marble-topped tables. (Equally startling and evocative is the noise of scores of mah-jongg players in Hongkong, slapping down their 'tiles' with the gesture of proud defiance shown by poor and humble men the world over when a high card gives them a fleeting sense of power.) Even the sight of a box of dominoes revives in me that moment of unreasoning fear in Segovia, more than half a century ago.

The origin of dominoes? Unknown. The origin of the name? Also unknown, for I cannot accept the theory put forward in *Le Code des Jeux** that the game was popular in the monasteries and that some monk, unduly anxious to win, called upon the deity for help. (If he did so, then his knowledge of Latin grammar must have been even

* Op. cit.

less than mine, which is absurd.) 'Domino' was also the cape or hood worn by priests in winter, from which, rather deviously, one came to the cloak and mask formerly so popular at fancy-dress balls.

Dominoes is yet one more game which may have been invented in China. In one form or another, it seems to have been played also by the Hebrews and the Greeks, and to have reached Italy in the sixteenth century and the rest of continental Europe more than a century later. Joseph Strutt,* with his customary priggishness, wrote that dominoes was 'a very childish sport, imported from France a few years back, and could have nothing but novelty to recommend it to the notice of grown persons in this country'. I suspect that he never played *'matador'* with grown persons in Spain.

* Op. cit.

CHAPTER TWELVE

The Antiquity of Board Games

*Board games in Egypt · The game of goose · The history of backgammon
· 'The national game of Africa' · Noughts and crosses and the Egyptians
· Nine men's morris · Bingo and housey-housey*

I HAVE written, in an earlier chapter, about chess, the
most important of all board games—so called because they have to be played on some flat surface,
generally of wood or cardboard. I have also written
about dice, which supply the motive power for so many
of them. Even in the early forms of chess, it will be remembered, dice were thrown to decide which piece
should be moved; it was not until dice, or astragals—the
knuckle-bones from the hind-legs of cloven-footed animals—had been abandoned that chess became the only
game in which luck plays no part.

That, of course, is the unfortunate part of the game
for most of us. More than a thousand years ago, the
Caliph Mamun transferred from chess to a game called
nard so that he could blame the dice, and most of us, to
maintain our own self-respect, have to call attention to
the malevolence of Dame Fortune. Did anyone, we protest, ever draw such rotten cards? (The answer, of
course, is in the affirmative, but the question is only a
rhetorical one, expecting no answer.) So we turn to one
or other of the board games, including some of the
oldest in the world, which depend upon the dice.

The earliest known board for a game with cells and
conical pieces to move in them, according to Murray,*
was found near Abydos, Upper Egypt, in a cemetery
dating back to between 4000 and 3000 B.C. In tombs of

* Op. cit.

the ninth to twelfth dynasties, boards have been found for a game known as dogs and jackals, which was a race game with some relationship to our nursery snakes and ladders and to the more complicated and popular French games of *le jeu de l'oie* and *le nain jaune*–both games for children which were adopted by grown-ups as excuses for betting.

In the seventeenth and eighteenth centuries, the *jeu de l'oie* was a favourite game among French adults, for whose benefit it was claimed that it had been 'revived' from the Greeks. But the cynics suggested that this association with Greece was only a publicity stunt, Hellenism then being very fashionable. The game, as played by generations of French children, seems to have been invented in Florence, during the rule of Francesco de' Medici (1541–1609), who passed it on to Philip II of Spain. Under the less impressive name of the game of goose, it reached England at the end of the century. The card or board on which it is played shows a kind of race course divided into sixty-three sections. One's advances, losses of turn or retreats are decided by the dice and, as in many other games, from darts in the inn to horse races on board ship, victory goes to the player who throws the exact number that will take him into the winning section.

The *jeu de l'oie* is interesting above all for the nature of the obstacles or advantages with which the player is met–nothing so simple as the head of a snake or the bottom rung of a ladder. They include a porcupine, a garden rake, a child bowling a hoop, a bottle with a glass, a lion, a mill, a well, a top, a canon, a church, an artist's palette, a prison, a ship, and a bugle. Every ninth section has a goose, which doubles the throw of the player lucky enough to land there. I have seen variants of the game based on French heraldry or geography. This is yet one more game that is played 'widdershins', or anti-clockwise—a direction generally associated, in a rather sinister way, with the East. It is also one more game which Napoleon liked to play; in this, as in his other games, he was a bad loser and his cheating was notorious.

In most of the early race games, the board seems to have consisted either of thirty-six cells, in three rows of twelve each, or in twenty cells, twelve of which are in three rows of four each, whereas the remaining eight project from the middle row down the whole length of the board. From one of these games we get backgammon and the French get *tric-trac*. One early version of the game is supposed to have been invented by Artaxerxes, King of Persia in the third century B.C. Another version was the Roman game of *ludus duodecim scriptorum*, and its boards, with three rows of twelve cells, have been found in many parts of Europe that formerly belonged to the Roman Empire. (Even more popular among Roman legionaries was a 'war-game' called *ludus latrunculorum* which was played on a kind of chess board and generally with pieces rather like our draughtsmen, but which, in Murray's opinion, is not the parent of draughts.)

A very popular modification of *ludus duodecim scriptorum* was called *tabula*—it was a *tabula* board that the Emperor Claudius had fixed inside his carriage to lessen the monotony of journeys over the bumpy Roman roads. In the twelfth century, Western Europe developed an enthusiasm for a game called tables, which closely resembled both the Roman *tabula* but with two rows of cells instead of three, and the Moslem game called *nard*, which was played on a backgammon board and to which the Caliph Mamum turned instead of chess. For many years tables was second in importance only to chess, and every self-respecting inn-keeper had boards at the service of his customers. In the early years of the seventeenth century, tables became backgammon.

Arguments about the origin of the name, back-gammon, are fierce and unconvincing. One version is that it comes from two Saxon words, meaning, respectively, back and game–since each player seeks to bring back his own men from the opponent's side of the board to his own. It seems a little strange that a game which reached England from Italy and France should have a Saxon name. But even stranger–at least to those of us who are not Welsh–is the Welsh claim that the name comes from 'bach', meaning 'little' and 'cam-maun', meaning 'battle'.

Strutt, who disapproved of so many games, had nothing to say against backgammon. Indeed, he claimed that it has 'always been considered a particularly respectable kind of amusement, quite fitting for country rectors, and not derogatory to the dignity of even higher functionaries of the Church'.

Mancala is a game of which most of us have probably never heard. I, for one, had not done so until I began to write this book. And yet it is classed as 'the national game of Africa' by none other than Edmond Hoyle (and here I must intervene with a few sentences in parenthesis about this greatest of all students of games. His *Encyclopaedia of Games* was first published in 1742, but so many enthusiastic editors have brought his book up to date that I should think at least half the games referred to in recent editions must have been invented since his death. The edition which I have consulted is the Goren edition, published in New York in 1950, and among other useful information, it works out in detail the mathematical odds against you if you become involved in most gambling games. After studying the tables of odds, I can almost convince myself that I could walk past the Casino at Monte Carlo without succumbing to, or even experiencing, the temptation to enter its imposing doorway.)

But mancala? Hoyle gives the game fifteen different names, of which this is the Arabic one, and says that it is played in both Africa and South-east Asia. The board has two parallel rows of six holes—two parallel rows of hollows in the sand or dust will do just as well—and either 72 or 84 small counters, beans, cowries, pebbles or what have you. Each player, starting from one hole in his side of the board, 'sows' its contents, one by one, in the successive holes (moving in an anti-clockwise direction, and thus suggesting the Asian origin of the game). There are so many varieties of mancala that I make no attempt to say what happens then, except that the position of the hole in which the 'sowing' ends probably decides whether the player wins the counters in the corresponding hole on the enemy's side of the board or loses an equivalent number to his enemy.

In one form or another, this game is played, especially in Moslem countries, from South-east Asia, throughout the countries bordering on the Indian Ocean, across Africa and to all those countries on the American continent to which African slaves were brought. It existed in Egypt more than 1,200 years B.C., and one imagines that it was spread in Africa by Arab traders in slaves and ivory, whose dhows sailed down the east coast of that continent with each north-east monsoon. But Dr Leakey, Kenya's famous anthropologist and stout defender of Africa's high place in human history, claims that some mancala boards in Kenya date back to neolithic times. It is clearly one of the oldest and also one of the most widely-played games in the world, and boards have been found carved in the stones from the Pyramid of Menkaura at Gizeh, in a cave in Ceylon and in Surinam, in South America.

One would not expect noughts and crosses to have much of a pedigree. But boards for a very similar 'game of alinement' (as Murray calls them) have been found, scratched or carved on some flat stone in Egypt, Crete, Greece and Rome, and one variety was played in China some five centuries before Christ. In these 'games of alinement' the aim is to get three or more of one's pieces in a row. The three-in-a-row game was played even in the holy city of Mecca, and was brought by the Moors into Spain, where it became known as *alquerque*, but in other Romance languages and in English the name was taken from the Latin for a counter or token, *merellus*. Thus the English variant of noughts and crosses was generally known as 'merels'. But it was also known as 'tick-tat-toe'–'tik-tak-tol' in Holland and 'tripp-trapp-trull' in Sweden, and it survives in the 'fruit machines' or 'one-armed bandits' in which so many of us have lost our sixpences. 'Three men's morris', which came to Britain with the Norman conquerors, was a more sophisticated version of noughts and crosses (which the second player cannot possibly win unless the first player has made a stupid mistake) in that it was played with pieces on a board, and not by noughts and crosses drawn on a slate or a piece of paper, and each player could try to make up a row by moving a piece one step along any line. Boards drawn or scratched on cloister seats or old desks in or near several English cathedrals–Canterbury, Gloucester, Norwich, Salisbury and Westminster Abbey–prove that at one time the game was very popular. Even more so were the larger merels–nine, eleven or twelve men's morris–and traces of several such games can still be found on the 'Pavement' in Jerusalem, where Pilate handed Jesus over to the Jews for crucifixion. Twelve men's morris was taken to America by the early English settlers.

These games of alinement were–and, in many cases, still are–played in almost every part of Asia, Europe and Africa. In America, various Indian tribes seem to have learnt to play games of this kind from the early *conquistadores.* Apparently they were also popular in China at the time of Confucius, and twenty-one books about them were written during the Swei-shu dynasty (A.D. 581–617). *'Bonus Socius'* ('The Good Companion')—an unidentified benefactor who produced the first known collection of chess problems in the thirteenth century—thought sufficiently highly of merels to add twenty-four merels and eleven dice problems to his collection. From the fourteenth century onwards, merels were so widely played that many boards were made for backgammon on one side and chess and merels on the other.

I summarise, rather shamelessly, Murray's conclusions as to the main sources of board games. In the third millennium B.C. 'what are essentially the same games' were being played in the lower valleys of the Nile, the Tigris and the Euphrates. In the second millennium, with the westward spread of civilisation, the main source was the eastern Mediterranean and, rather later, Greece itself. The first evidence of board games in northern India dates back to about 500 B.C., and these games spread to Persia and—probably carried by Buddhists—to China. Considerably later, the Chinese exported these games to Japan and South-east Asia.

In the first millennium, the Greeks occupied Sicily and southern Italy, and naturally they took their games with them. Then, over a long period, Roman soldiers in remote parts of their empire and Islamic invaders in Spain and Sicily taught new games to new people. Several of these games first reached Britain not through the French, as one might have expected, but through the Scandinavians, who had come into contact with the Romans in what is now Germany. Finally, the Europeans—especially the Spanish, the British, the French and the Dutch—took their games with them on the perilous voyage across the Atlantic. I mentioned in the

first chapter their surprise on seeing the American Indians playing with balls made of rubber; they also found
that certain board games already existed. The Mexicans, for example, had a game slightly resembling the
Indian game of *pachisi*, the ancestor of the modern game
of ludo. Both games were played on a cruciform board.
The early Egyptians sometimes threw staves instead of
dice or astragals—some were found in Tutenkhamen's
tomb. So did the Mexicans—if the three staves fell with
their rounded sides upwards, the player scored ten and
had another throw; no round sides upwards gave him five;
two gave him three; one gave him two. (There was
thus not much difference in scoring between a game
played by the Mexicans before the arrival of Cortes and
the Swedish game with a matchbox which I described
in the second chapter.) But, despite these superficial
similarities, Murray doubts whether any Asian games
did, in fact, reach America before they were taken there
by Europeans. The games of American Indians seem to
be more divinatory in origin than the games of Asia and
Europe, which is not astonishing, since most games
originated with pagan beliefs and superstitions, and
what we like to call civilisation has reached the American
Indians later than the peoples of Asia and Europe. Incidentally, Murray suggests that possibly the Eskimos,
the Australian aborigines and the natives of New
Guinea are the only peoples that have no native board
games.

*   *   *

And then there's bingo, better known to people who
travel in ships as housey-housey and to people two
centuries ago as *lotto* (which must not be confused with
the Italian '*lotto*' of today—a state-run numbers game—
whereas the Anglo-American bingo is known in Italy as
la tombola). At the time of writing, the game still fills

halls and cinemas all over Britain, often with staid, middle-class ladies who were taught when they were young that actresses were always immoral, that novels should not be read on Sundays, that women should ride horses side-saddle, that one ought not to dance more than twice or three times with the same man at a ball, and that they should not smoke or drink whisky in public. *Time* magazine tells me that bingo is still forbidden in the State of Virginia, so that people who want to play have to call it beano, bungo or lotto.

Known as housey-housey or tombola – taken from the Italian, but with the accent misplaced in the process – the game has been played on ships for many years; its sudden success throughout Britain in the nineteen-sixties is one of the most fantastic illustrations of the fever for gambling that is apt to overtake a nation during a time of uncertainty about the future. Since it calls for alertness of mind and eye, the old ladies who like it but who dislike gambling manage to convince themselves that it does not come in that category – just as many teetotallers manage to convince themselves that cider is not alcoholic. (A pint of home-brewed Somersetshire cider might give them doubts, but they prefer the sweet, bottled stuff which, they argue, is exciting because it's fizzy but non-alcoholic because it's sweet.)

Bingo is an old game, which is said to have been invented by a Genoese nobleman, Benedetto Gentile, and to have been brought back to France by the troops of Francis I, early in the sixteenth century. One curious feature of the game is that, in France as well as in Britain, many of the numbers have nicknames. Just as 66 is known as 'clicketty click' and zero becomes 'Kelly's eye' in the British game, in France, 11 becomes '*les deux jambes*' ('legs eleven' accompanied by wolf whistles, in England), 33 becomes '*les deux bossus*', 69 becomes '*bout-çi, bout-là*', and 57 becomes '*misère en*

Prusse', allegedly in memory of a devastating defeat of the French at the hands of the Prussians at Rossbach in 1757. (So one might argue that bingo, or at least the French version of it, helps to polish up one's history.)

*　　*　　*

And with bingo, I finish. I have written about only a few of the many thousands of ways in which men and women and children throughout the centuries have kept themselves amused. But I have written enough to be astonished by the number of games that began as religious rites. And so, I suppose, it should be, for even in their debased, modern forms they have an important part in the development of civilisation.

Professor Huizinga, to whose *Homo Ludens* I have referred in earlier chapters, attaches very great value to the 'play' element in the human make-up, and not only because it trains people to exercise self-control, because it develops a wider loyalty, because it sublimates aggressive tendencies, because it restores a sense of balance and proportion to those who tend to work too hard and in too limited a sector. There is all that, and more.

'Play', he writes, 'is older than culture, for culture, however inadequately defined, always presupposes human society, and animals have not waited for man to teach them their playing. . . . Young dogs keep to the rule that you shall not bite, or not bite hard, your brother's ear. They pretend to get terribly angry. And —what is most important—in all these doings they plainly experience tremendous fun and enjoyment.' He could have gone much lower down the scale than dogs to show how universal is the 'play' element; I have watched minnow-sized fish in both the Lake of Geneva and the Lago Maggiore queueing up to jump over a tiny floating twig, and I presume I could have watched other fish behaving in this way in other lakes if the climate had been equally encouraging to idleness on a lake-side bench.

'Even in its simplest form on animal level', writes the Professor, 'play is more than a mere physiological phenomenon or a psychological reflex. . . . It is a significant function—that is to say, there is some sense to it.' So perhaps there is also some sense to a book about the past of pastimes.

Bibliography

Aberdare, Lord *The Story of Tennis* (Stanley Paul, London, 1959)

Aubrey, John *The Natural History of Wiltshire* (London, 1671)

Aveline, Claude *Le Code des Jeux* (Hachette, Paris, 1961)

Becq de Fouquières *Les Jeux des Anciens* (Paris, 1869)

Bett, Henry *The Games of Children* (Methuen, London, 1929)

Bird, H. E. *Chess History and Reminiscences* (Dean, London, 1893)

Bled, Victor du *Histoire Anecdotique et Psychologique des Jeux de Cartes* (Paris, 1919)

Boorde, Andrew *Dyetery of Health* (1547)

Brooke, Iris *Pleasures of the Past* (Odhams, London, 1955)

Burton, Robert *Anatomy of Melancholy* (London, 1621)

Campbell, Sir Guy *A History of Golf in Great Britain* (Cassell, London, 1952)

Cardus, Neville *English Cricket* (Collins, London, 1945)

Carew, R. *Survey of Cornwall*, 1602

Castiglione, Baldassare *The Courtier* (Venice, 1528)

Chatto, William A. *Facts and Speculations on the Origin and History of Playing Cards* (Russell Smith, London, 1848)

Clark, Robert *Golf, a Royal and Ancient Game* (Macmillan, London, 1893)

Cleaver, Hylton *Sporting Rhapsody* (Hutchinson, London, 1951)

Cotton, Charles *The Compleat Gamester* (London, 1674)

Cullin, Stewart *Games of North American Indians* (Washington, 1907)

Daiken, L. *Children's Games Throughout the Year* (Batsford, London, 1949)

Dale, T. F. *Polo, Past and Present* (Country Life, London, 1905)

Davidsohn, Robert *Firenze ai Tempi di Dante* (Florence, 1929)

Dini, Vittorio & Magrini, Florildo *Gli Antichi Sporte e i Giuochi Popolari* (Arezzo, 1966)

Douglas, Norman *London Street Games* (Chatto & Windus, London, 1916)

Falkener, E. *Games Ancient and Oriental and How to Play Them* (Longmans Green, London, 1892)

BIBLIOGRAPHY

Finn, T. *The Watney Book of Pub Games* (Queen Anne Press, London, 1967)

Fiske, Willard *Chess in Iceland* (Florence, 1905)

Fitzstephen, William *Description of London* (twelfth century)

Fraser, Antonia *A History of Toys* (Weidenfeld & Nicolson, London, 1966)

Gomme, Alice *The Traditional Games of England, Scotland and Ireland* (London, 1894)

Gosson, Stephen *The School of Abuse* (1579)

Hall, Christina *English Sports and Pastimes* (Batsford, London, 1949)

Hall, D. J. *English Mediaeval Pilgrimage* (Routledge & Kegan Paul, London, 1965)

Hoyle, Edmond *Encyclopaedia of Games* (Goren, New York, 1950)

Huizinga, J. *Homo Ludens* (Routledge, London, 1949)

Jesse, J. Henaege *Memoirs of the Court of England during the Reign of the Stuarts* (Bentley, London, 1840)

Klahre, Alfred *Chess Potpourri* (Brooklyn, New York, 1931)

Knight's London (London, 1841)

Lang, Andrew *Cricket* (in the Badminton Library, London, 1893)

Marcolini, Francesco *Le Sorti* (Venice, 1540)

Markham, Gervase *Pleasures of Princes* (London, 1635)

Mahttews, Henry *Diary of an Invalid* (Murray, London, 1820)

Monckton, O. Paul *Pastimes in Times Past* (West Strand Publishing Co., London, 1913)

Morley, H. T. *Old and Curious Playing Cards* (Batsford, London, 1931)

Murray, H. J. R. *A History of Board Games other than Chess* (Clarendon Press, Oxford, 1952)

Oliff, John *The Romance of Wimbledon* (Hutchinson, London, 1949)

Pole, W. *Handbook of Games* (George Bell, London, 1890)

Richter, W. *Jeux des Grecs et des Romains* (Paris, 1891)

Strutt, J. *Sports and Pastimes of the People of England* (Tegg, London, 1838)

Taylor, E. S. *History of Playing Cards* (John Camden Hotten, London, 1865)

Van der Linde, A. *Geschichte und Litteratur des Schachspiele* (Berlin, 1870)

Index

INDEX

INDEX

INDEX

Lawn tennis: claims for invention of, 36; explanation of scoring strokes, 39; popularity in America, 41

Leapfrog, 62

Le jeu de l'oie, board game, 144-5

Le nain jaune, board game, 144

Leisure time, problems of, 11-13

Liar dice, 26

Loggats, bowling game, 128

London Bridge, children's game, 57, 62

Lord, Thomas, 52

Lord's cricket ground, 52

Lotto, numbers game, 150

Louis X, King; 'real' tennis player, 31

Louis XV, King; 'real' tennis player, 31

Ludo, 150

Ludus duodecim scriptorum, board game, 145

Ludus latrunculorum, board game, 91-2, 145

Ludum pilae celebrem, ball game, 95

Lydians, credited with inventions of pastimes, 14

Mah-jongg, 141

Mancala, board game, 146-7

Marbles, 62, 64-5, 138

Markham, Gervase, 100-1; Works, *Pleasures of Princes*, 101q.

Martial, Marcus Valerius, 62-3

Marylebone Cricket Club, 40; authority of, 52

Matador, 142

'Matchbox' dice, *see* Dice

Matthews, Henry, 53; Works, *Diary of an Invalid*, 53q.

May-pole, 59-60, 66

Mazarin, Cardinal, 119; one of greatest gamblers in history, 116-17

Medici, Francesco de', 144; inventor of *le jeu de l'oie*, 144-5

Merels, also known as 'noughts and crosses', 148-9

Merlin, Joseph, inventor of roller skates, 135

Mississippi, form of billiards, 132-3

Moore, Henry, 45; player of 'old cat', 45

Mora, game of, 28; variety of, 28

Morris dancing, 51, 65-6

Murray, H. J. R.; conclusions on board games, 149-50; theories regarding invention of chess, 84-5

Musical chairs, 63

'Mustering', rural recreation, 103

My birdie whistles, children's game, 62

Naibbe, or *naibi*, name by which cards first known in Italy, 108-9

Naipes, Spanish name for playing cards, 115

Naismith, James, inventor of basketball, 43-4

Nard, board game, 143, 145

Nine Holes, bowling game, 128

Noughts and crosses, 147-8; alternative name for, 148

'Nuts in May', 58-9

'Old cat', field game, 44-5

Olympic Games, 67-70; abolition of, 68; continuance of, 69-70; institution of, 68

Oranges and Lemons, 63-4

Orisippos, first naked competitor in Olympic Games, 68

Outerbridge, Miss, pioneer of lawn tennis in America, 41

Pachisi, board game, 150

Paganica, slight resemblance to golf, 74

Palamedes, attributed inventor of dice, 19, 24, 81

Pall mall, 75; rules of, 42-3

Paterson, John, 76

Penneech, card game, 122

Pepys, Samuel, 34-5, 43

Pharaon, card game, 120

Philometer, attributed inventor of chess, 79-80

Piling the donkey, children's game, 62

Ping-pong, *see* Table tennis

Piquet, 120

Poker, 119-20

Polish banker, children's game, 62

Polo, 16, 129-30; ground dimensions, equipment, rules of, 129-30; Persia as home of, 129-30

Poque, card game, 119

Primero, Spanish card game, 118-19

Prisoner's base, children's game, 63

Queen Anne, children's game, 62

Queen Nazareen, card game, 122

Raps on the bugle, children's game, 62

'Real' or 'royal' tennis, 30: court layout, 35-6; decree forbidding playing of by lower classes, 32; played by monarchs, 31-2; reaches England, 33

Ring games, 59

Robertson, Allan, golf-ball maker, 15

159

INDEX